Central Banking
after the Great Recession

Central Banking
after the Great Recession
Lessons Learned, Challenges Ahead

David Wessel, editor

BROOKINGS INSTITUTION PRESS
Washington, D.C.

The Brookings Institution is a private nonprofit organization devoted to research, education, and publication on important issues of domestic and foreign policy. Its principal purpose is to bring the highest quality independent research and analysis to bear on current and emerging policy problems. Interpretations or conclusions in Brookings publications should be understood to be solely those of the authors.

Library of Congress Cataloging-in-Publication data is available.
ISBN 978-0-8157-2608-1 (pbk. : alk. paper)

9 8 7 6 5 4 3 2 1

Printed on acid-free paper

Typeset in Sabon

Composition by Cynthia Stock
Silver Spring, Maryland

CONTENTS

ACKNOWLEDGMENTS

In addition to the authors and panelists who contributed to our January 16, 2014, event and are prominently mentioned elsewhere, this book represents the hard work of several other individuals. Alison Hope was a careful and patient copy editor of the original papers. Emily Parker diligently winnowed the proceedings of the conference into digestible morsels. With her usual skill and energy, DJ Nordquist helped orchestrate both the conference and the subsequent publication of the papers and book. At the Brookings Institution Press, thanks go to Valentina Kalk, director, Larry Converse, production manager, and Janet Walker, managing editor, for seeing the book through its final stages. *Central Banking after the Great Recession* is the first book to come from the work of the Hutchins Center on Fiscal and Monetary Policy at Brookings, which is supported by the Hutchins Family Foundation.

1

INTRODUCTION

DAVID WESSEL

The January 2014 inaugural event of the Hutchins Center on Fiscal and Monetary Policy at the Brookings Institution focused on lessons that the Federal Reserve and other central banks have—or should have—learned from the most severe financial crisis the world economy has weathered in seventy-five years. The session was an encouraging beginning toward our goals of increasing public understanding of fiscal and monetary policy and improving the quality and efficacy of those policies. As Brookings President Strobe Talbott said in his introductory remarks:

> Monetary and fiscal policies are the purview of different parts of the federal government, but they have in common two goals: easing our economic woes, particularly the persistence of high unemployment, while at the same time ensuring that decisions that we make today on spending, taxes, interest rates, and financial regulation lay the foundations for a better life for our children and grandchildren.
>
> That means fiscal and monetary policies need to be consistent and compatible if we are to accelerate our recovery from the recent crisis and ensure a healthy economic future. This is a classic challenge to the Brookings mission, which is contributing to the improvement of our system of governance. It's an opportunity to apply the Brookings method which is to convene the best experts;

pose the right questions; marshal relevant facts; generate innovative, pragmatic, actionable ideas; debate their merits in a civil, constructive, nonpartisan fashion; engage the public, the private sector, and the policy community, and then advocate for sound policy.

Glenn Hutchins, whose family foundation provided the gift that created the Hutchins Center, added,

At Brookings we are uncompromising in our zeal to protect and promote the independence of our scholars. This is because we are committed to producing only the very highest quality, most data-driven, most rigorous research humanly possible. And we fundamentally believe that can only be accomplished when our scholars are absolutely free to pursue their research to its logical conclusion without ideological or financial fear or favor.

In that spirit, we asked John Williams, president of the Federal Reserve Bank of San Francisco, to reflect on lessons he has gleaned from the past five years of extraordinary, unconventional monetary policy. He said central bankers should not assume, as they once did, that episodes in which short-term interest rates fall to zero will be infrequent or short-lived. In his view, the Fed's experiments with "forward guidance"—promising to keep rates low for a long time—and with large-scale purchases of bonds and mortgages ("quantitative easing") have been successful, although he acknowledged that quantifying their efficacy has proved difficult. He highlighted three unresolved issues:

—Should central banks shift from inflation targets to price-level or nominal GDP-level targets?

—Should large-scale asset purchases be a standard tool of monetary policy, and if so, how should they be implemented?

—Is the 2 percent inflation target in common use by central banks high enough?

We then turned to an occasional critic of the Fed, Martin Feldstein of Harvard University. He broadened the discussion to inadequacy of fiscal policy, which, he said, put too much burden on the Fed during and immediately following the crisis. We invited Paul Tucker, now at Harvard University after serving as deputy governor for financial stability of the Bank of England, to identify where postcrisis reforms for the financial system have gone far enough—and where they haven't. He had praise for the strengthened regulation of banks but warned that too little has been done to address risks posed by financial markets. He outlined the new approach being followed in the United States and elsewhere to protect taxpayers from paying for future bank bailouts while preserving financial stability in the face of failure. That approach essentially requires the bank-holding companies to hold enough equity and debt to absorb any losses at their subsidiaries and be reconstituted immediately as going concerns. That approach essentially requires the bank-holding companies issue enough equity and long-term debt so that the parent company—as opposed to taxpayers—can absorb any banking losses. Rodgin Cohen of Sullivan & Cromwell, one of the leading banking lawyers, was concerned about the international complications involved in resolving global institutions, and he offered a few modifications to Paul Tucker's proposal.

We also asked our colleague Donald Kohn, a former Federal Reserve vice chairman, to assess the risks to the Fed's independence in the wake of the crisis. In his view, the risks are substantial and unwelcome because politically independent central banks have been proven to be an essential bulwark against inflation. In responding, Christina Romer of the University of California at Berkeley argued that the main reason to shield central banks from political interference is not to resist inflation, but because monetary policy made by experts is better than policy made by politicians. The biggest threat to that independence, she said, comes from bad monetary policy decisions. Kenneth Rogoff of Harvard University was more sympathetic to Kohn's view and expressed concern that today's environment is one in which central bank independence could prove very difficult to preserve.

All this provided substantial fodder for thinking and rethinking the recent past and offered an agenda for future research and policy. That alone would have been fruitful, but we concluded with an illuminating interview with Ben Bernanke, then in his final weeks as chairman of the Federal Reserve, by Liaquat Ahamed, a Brookings trustee and author of the Pulitzer Prize–winning *Lords of Finance: The Bankers Who Broke the World*.

Perhaps the most telling moment came when Ahamed recalled that then-Treasury Secretary Tim Geithner once referred to Ben Bernanke as the "Buddha of central bankers"—and asked if Bernanke had suffered any sleepless nights during the crisis. Bernanke said he had, adding, "It was kind of like if you're in a car wreck. You're mostly involved in trying to avoid going off the bridge, and then later on you say, 'Oh, my God. . . .'"

This volume includes a lightly edited transcript of that conversation as well as the reflections of Williams, Tucker, and Kohn and the wide-ranging discussion with the panelists and the audience that followed. You can keep track of the evolution of the Hutchins Center on Fiscal and Monetary Policy on the website: www.brookings.edu/hutchinscenter.

2

A CONVERSATION WITH BEN BERNANKE
Liaquat Ahamed and Ben Bernanke

Two weeks before the end of his eight-year term as chairman of the Federal Reserve, Ben Bernanke was interviewed by Liaquat Ahamed, a Brookings trustee and author of the Pulitzer Prize–winning *Lords of Finance: The Bankers Who Broke the World*. As Glenn Hutchins noted in introducing the conversation, Ahamed's book was about the mistakes that central bankers made during the Great Depression. The story of Ben Bernanke's tenure is about the steps the Federal Reserve took to avoid another Great Depression. An edited transcript of the conversation follows.

AHAMED: The way you handled the financial crisis in 2008 will clearly go down as one of your signature achievements. You've said somewhere that the playbook that you relied on was essentially given by a British economist in the 1860s, Walter Bagehot.[1] His dictum was that in a financial crisis, the central bank should lend unlimited amounts to solvent institutions against good collateral at a penalty rate. How useful in practice was that rule in guiding you?

BERNANKE: It was excellent advice. This was the advice that's been used by central banks going back to at least the 1700s. When you have a market or a financial system that is short of liquidity and there's a lack of confidence, a panic, then the central bank is the lender of last resort. It's the institution that can provide the cash liquidity to calm the panic

---

1. See http://research.stlouisfed.org/publications/es/09/ES0907.pdf.

and to make sure that depositors and other short-term lenders are able to get their money.

In the context of the crisis of 2008, the main difference was that the financial system that we have today obviously looked very different in its details, if not in its conceptual structure, from what Walter Bagehot saw in the nineteenth century. And so the challenge for us at the Fed was to adapt Bagehot's advice to the context of a modern financial system. So, for example, instead of having retail depositors standing in line outside the doors, as was the case in the 1907 panic, in the United States we had runs by wholesale short-term lenders like repo lenders or commercial-paper lenders, and we had to find ways to essentially provide liquidity to stop those runs.

So it was a different institutional context, but very much an approach that was entirely consistent, I think, with Bagehot's recommendations.

AHAMED: Now in addition to lending to institutions, you intervened in markets. Is there a sort of similarly pithy dictum, a Bernanke rule that you can come up with about when the Fed should intervene in markets and when it shouldn't?

BERNANKE: If we're talking about the crisis period, I would say that all the interventions we did fit under the Bagehot heading. For example, the commercial-paper facility that we set up was essentially designed to prevent a run on this particular form of financing. It was a different institutional structure, but it was, again, essentially the same Bagehot rule being applied in a different institutional context. So while the analogies between what we did and the run on the savings and loan in *It's a Wonderful Life* are not always obvious, there was, in fact, a very close parallel.

Now we have done other interventions, with our asset purchase program, for example, but that I would call those the monetary policy part of our response.

AHAMED: The crisis began in August of 2007, when there was a problem with a fund run by a French bank.[2] And if you trace through it, it actually continued until the spring of 2009. So that was a long time. And despite major intervention after Lehman, despite the Troubled Asset Repurchase Program (TARP), you still had a run on Citibank,

---

2. See http://www.nytimes.com/2007/08/10/business/worldbusiness/09cnd-eurobank.html?_r=1&.

you still had a run on Bank of America. Why did it take so long to get it under control?

BERNANKE: It was not a continuous crisis of equal intensity for the entire period that you described. In the fall of 2007, we were seeing obviously a lot of stress in markets, but at that point, it was not obvious whether this was going to be the start of something bigger or whether it was something more comparable, say, to some of the disruptions we had seen in the 1990s, for example, around the Russian debt crisis.

There was a critical point in March of 2008 with the Bear Stearns episode, and that was a period of very intense stress in the repo markets and in some other parts of the financial markets. After Bear Stearns, financial conditions calmed fairly notably for a while. Obviously we remained very alert. The Federal Reserve was beginning to supervise the investment banks together with the Securities and Exchange Commission over the summer. So we were not complacent about the crisis being over, but conditions were certainly more stable after Bear Stearns for a number of months. And there was, you know, at least some hope— given that, for example, the Bush administration was undertaking a fiscal expansionary policy—that things might calm. But, again, we were very attentive.

The real intense phase, I think everyone would agree, began with the takeover, the putting into conservatorship of Fannie Mae and Freddie Mac in early September of 2008. And that was followed by this very intense period of Lehman and AIG, the TARP, and so on. So the very intense period from, say, September 1 until the latter part of the year, that was the period of greatest stress and greatest risk.

And the combination of our lending programs and the injection of government capital, the fiscal aspect of that, brought the crisis down considerably by the end of the year. Of course, into the next year we were still working to stabilize the system with our stress testing, addressing some concerns of specific institutions with our monetary policy and the like, but I don't think it's fair to characterize the crisis as being something that was continuous for a year and a half. Rather, there were periods of ebbs and flows.

And in the most intense period in September and October, I think we actually got that under control reasonably quickly with the combination of the Fed's liquidity provision, the TARP, the fiscal injections, plus actions by the FDIC [Federal Deposit Insurance Corporation] and other agencies as well.

AHAMED: Hank Paulson describes having sleepless nights at that time, you know, agonizing that he would go down in history as the Herbert Hoover of this episode. And I think Tim Geithner once described you as the Buddha of central banks, which implies a certain level of enlightened detachment.[3] Now, did you have sleepless nights?

BERNANKE: Oh, sure, absolutely. But it's my nature, I think, to kind of focus on the problem, and I was so absorbed in what was happening and trying to find a response to it that I wasn't really in that kind of reflective mode. It was kind of like if you're in a car wreck. You're mostly involved in trying to avoid going off the bridge; and then later on you say, "Oh, my God. . . ."

AHAMED: Your partnership with Secretary Paulson and then Secretary Geithner was clearly central to solving the crisis. To an outsider it's remarkable what a united front you presented, but you did have different backgrounds, different personalities, and represented different arms of government. And so to some degree there's a natural tension. The central bank does liquidity. The Treasury does solvency. But the distinction is not always very clear. Were there any big disagreements?

MR. BERNANKE: You're absolutely right that we had a very strong partnership: Hank Paulson, Tim Geithner, and me. We are different people, different backgrounds. And I think we were actually quite complementary in various ways. And we certainly all recognized the seriousness of the situation and the need for cooperation among the Treasury, the Fed, and other agencies. And that was the overwhelming imperative: to work together to try to solve the problem.

There were certainly points where we were trying to address the financial condition of AIG or some other politically very difficult problem, and there was a little bit of discussion about whether or not the Fed or the Treasury should take the lead on that particular area. But in the end, Paulson, in particular, who during the heat of the 2008 crisis, was the person who was most exposed to the political winds, because as secretary of the Treasury, he represented the administration and he

---

3. See http://www.washingtonpost.com/blogs/wonkblog/wp/2013/01/25/exclusive-geithners-private-farewell-to-obama-and-treasury-staff/.

had to go to Congress and so on. In the end, he always did what had to be done.

And I think that was the reason that we worked together: the combination of our complementary backgrounds and skills and the fact that we shared a common purpose. There were many people in the world, economists among them, who thought that it's perfectly safe to let the financial companies go down. We heard that even at Jackson Hole a few days before the crisis intensified in September of 2008. The three of us were all very much in agreement that that was not a wise thing to do, and we were committed to not doing that.

Let me just also say, though, that while the interventions with large failing firms are the part of the story that gets the most attention, and are the most controversial, much of the good work that was done was a little bit more under the radar and had to do with our actions to try to stabilize key financial markets like the money market funds, the commercial-paper market, the asset-backed securities market; to strengthen the commercial banking system and so on; and to work with our partners to do currency swaps with fourteen other central banks. There was a whole range of things that we did that didn't involve firm interventions, which were less visible, but probably occupied a much greater portion of our time and were at least as important if not more important in terms of stabilizing the system.

AHAMED: Now in David Wessel's book [*In Fed We Trust: Ben Bernanke's War on the Great Panic*] there's a scene where he has you sort of pushing Secretary Paulson to go to Congress. So if the Treasury had gone to Congress to get money earlier, could we have avoided Lehman?

BERNANKE: No, for the following reason: even with Lehman, even with the stock market tumbling, it took two votes of the House of Representatives to get the TARP approved. I remember a senator telling me, when we were trying to go around and explain to members of Congress why we needed the TARP and why it was critical to the stability of the American economy: "I have to tell you," he said, "my calls on this from my constituents are 50/50. It's 50 percent 'no' and 50 percent 'hell, no.'"

So it was a very unpopular policy. As Barney Frank has put it, it's one of the most successful government policies ever, and nevertheless one of the most unpopular. There was no chance that we could have gotten a TARP-type program before it was becoming evident how bad the situation was going to be, so that was the catch-22 we were in, basically. But it was also clear to me at that point in mid-September that the ad hoc interventions on which we had relied, given that we didn't really have a framework for resolving these firms, had reached their limit. And we had no choice but to involve Congress, and I was very clear about that.

AHAMED: Let's talk about that political backlash. Dodd-Frank, for example, while giving the Fed more power to prevent a crisis, limits the ability of the Fed to intervene in the way that it did in 2008. Can you tell us more about that? Are you worried about the consequences of that?

BERNANKE: No. We were supportive of those changes, were totally comfortable. What we're talking about here is the so-called 13(3) provisions, which allow the Fed to make emergency loans to individuals, partnerships, and corporations under certain conditions—unusual and exigent circumstances as it was called.[4] And we used those tools for the first time, essentially since the Great Depression, to support the collective effort of the government to prevent the collapse of some critical firms, as well as do broad-based lending in a number of key markets, as I was describing before.

The former, the interventions for firms, again, happened because there was no framework. There was nothing but the standard bankruptcy code. And the trouble with the bankruptcy code in this context is that what bankruptcy does first and foremost is defend the interest of the creditors, which is a great thing, but there's no recognition in the bankruptcy code that you also have to worry about the stability of the financial system. In any case, we didn't have anything like that in 2008.

So the Dodd-Frank Act, Title 2, created an orderly liquidation authority, which provided a much more structured and flexible approach to addressing a failing critical firm in the middle of a crisis.[5] So we don't need that authority anymore. We have tools now, which we didn't have before, to address individual firms. At the same time, the 13(3) rules in Dodd-Frank do permit a so-called broad-based program so that our actions with regard to the commercial paper, asset-backed securities, and some of the other markets that we provided liquidity to presumably

4. See http://www.federalreserve.gov/oig/files/FRS_Lending_Facilities_Report_final-11-23-10_web.pdf.
5. See http://www.law.cornell.edu/wex/dodd-frank_title_ii.

would still be legal, as would the primary dealer facility, which was open to all primary dealers.

So the key things that we did would still be possible, although we'd have to get the secretary of treasury's permission. And we're perfectly happy that there are alternative ways to deal with a failing firm and that the Fed doesn't have to intervene in the way we did in 2008.

AHAMED: Are you worried about the political backlash against the Fed, the consequences, both for monetary policy and how future Fed decisionmakers will be able to respond in a crisis?

BERNANKE: Well, first of all, it wasn't really a surprise. This is another place where history helps you. If you think about the 1930s, we had exactly, as you well know, the same kind of reaction. In fact, it was much more intense.

AHAMED: Well, no, those guys did the wrong thing; and you did the right thing. [Laughter]

BERNANKE: Well, it wasn't so much the Fed—the Fed did keep its head down in the '30s, unfortunately—but the government in general. There were marches on Washington and strong populist movements and serious talk about revolution even among some parts of the population. And, of course, what Roosevelt argued was that the strong actions he was taking were about saving capitalism essentially. It's not surprising in a sense that you would get this populist type of reaction.

I guess the only comment I would make is this: think about the alternative of not doing what the Fed did. The Fed was created to address financial panics. And its independence and its ability to act quickly is a key feature of what the Fed is about. And if we had not done that and if the financial system had imploded and the economy had plunged into even a deeper depression, I think the populist reaction would have been pretty bad as well. So we were kind of stuck one way or the other. So we did the right thing, I hope. We tried to do the right thing. And there certainly has been pushback.

We hope that as the economy improves, and as we tell our story, and as more information comes out about why we did what we did and so on, people will appreciate and understand that what we did was necessary, that it was in the interest of the broader public, it was a Main Street set of actions aimed at helping the average American. And as time passes and that becomes clearer, I'm hopeful that these political concerns will wane.

That being said, the reason the Fed is independent is so that it can take emergency actions or any other actions, policy actions, independent of short-run political pressures. And the day that we allow those short-run political pressures to make us do something that is not the right thing for the economy, then our independence at that point is effectively gone.

AHAMED: Let's move to monetary policy. In many ways you had a playbook for how to deal with the financial crisis. We heard from John Williams this morning that there was only a little bit of theory, some of which you had helped develop, but we were really operating blind. So in devising QE [quantitative easing] and all these other unconventional monetary policies, were you pretty confident that the theory would work?

BERNANKE: Well, the problem with QE is it works in practice, but it doesn't work in theory. But it's a bit of an exaggeration to say that this was all unprecedented. Obviously we had the case of Japan, and they had taken some of these actions. We had those experiences. We learned some things from the '30s and so on. I think of QE as being a basic monetarist principle, which is that these are some of the ideas that Friedman and Schwartz talked about, which is that the way you can stimulate the economy is by swapping liquid assets for less liquid assets.[6] That's essentially what an open market operation is.

On the side of forward guidance and so on, people like Michael Woodford and Paul Krugman and others had talked about those issues and how that would work.[7] So we were relying on research. Just let me say, parenthetically, that monetary policy in general is an extraordinary example of how thinking within a policy institution and in the academic world can mutually benefit each other. We made use of the ideas that we got from academia and also ideas that came from our own experiments.

The basic problem was that the short-term interest rate was effectively zero as of December 2008, and any analysis would suggest that that was not enough economic monetary support to achieve a sufficiently robust recovery. We needed additional stimulus. These were the

6. Milton Friedman and Anna Jacobson Schwartz, *A Monetary History of the United States, 1869–1960* (Princeton University Press, 1963).

7. For Woodford's comments, see http://www.columbia.edu/~mw2230/RiksbankIT. pdf; for Krugman's, see http://krugman.blogs.nytimes.com/2013/09/13/tobin-and-the-taper-wonkish/?.

two methods, with some experimentation, that we came to. I do think that they both have been helpful and we've learned a lot; but I would disagree that these are completely novel ideas.

A number of different central banks have tried various forms of forward guidance, and the Federal Reserve, even before the crisis, talked about keeping interest rates low for a considerable period. So what we were doing was trying to build on what others had already done.

AHAMED: Now, quantitative easing or QE was much more controversial than the lender-of-last-resort type of things that you did, and you had to deal with a fair number of skeptics, including within the FOMC [Federal Open Market Committee]. How did you persuade so many people to go along with it?

BERNANKE: I'm not sure I would agree with you. They both had elements of controversy. When we were looking for additional measures that we could take to provide additional accommodation and to help stabilize financial markets, some of the biggest measures we took were in late 2008, and then in March 2009, when we put in a very big program. And the beginning of that program was very broadly supported in the Federal Open Market Committee. It was felt that that intervention would both provide very much needed monetary policy support and would add to the liquidity of markets in general, which were still under great stress at that time. So the beginning of it was certainly a broadly supported idea.

Subsequently, that gave us the opportunity to see what the effects were and to do analysis and so on. And the staff analysis and pretty large literature that is out there has suggested that while there are differences in views about how effective QE is, the great majority of studies have found that it is at least somewhat effective. Given that we were at the limits of what conventional monetary policy could do, we felt that we needed to take additional steps. And for the most part it had been supported.

A number of the folks who have voted against it or have been critical of it have argued that perhaps it wasn't needed. I don't think that a large number of people on the committee feel that it's inherently not effective.

AHAMED: We know what the benefits are because they're lower long-term rates, lower mortgage rates, so what are the costs that you worry about?

BERNANKE: The costs that people talk about are not really costs. One cost that gets talked about is, oh, is this going to be inflationary? And while, of course, it's always possible for the Fed to raise rates too late or too early and so on, I think we have plenty of tools now at this point. We've developed all the tools we need to manage interest rates, to tighten monetary policy, even if the balance sheet stays where it is or gets bigger.

And because we can do that, that means that we can run monetary policy in the normal way and avoid any risks of undue inflation or other such problems. I don't think that's a concern, and those who've been saying, you know, for the past five years that we're just on a brink of hyperinflation: I would just point to this morning's consumer price index number and suggest that inflation is just not really a significant risk of this policy.

Another concern that people have talked about is the idea that the Fed might take capital losses. That, of course, is not impossible, but I would say that from a social point of view we have not only helped the economy already, but we've actually helped the fiscal situation quite significantly with hundreds of billions of dollars that we've remitted to the Treasury. And that doesn't even take into account the benefits for the public fisc of a stronger economy, more tax revenues, and the like. So that risk is, again, not a true social economic risk. If anything, it's a public relations risk for the Fed, perhaps, but it's not a serious economic risk.

The main risk that my colleagues have pointed to is various aspects of financial stability or potential for financial instability. There is always some concern that, really for any kind of easy monetary policy, after a period of time, there may be some reaching for yield or some misevaluation of assets. And given what happened, of course, just five years ago, we're extraordinarily sensitive to that risk.

Now, of course, that's really for different kinds of monetary policy. QE in addition works on term premiums to a significant extent, and we simply have less knowledge about how term premiums are determined, and therefore there's a little bit of additional concern about volatility associated with the management of QE.

So there are certainly some risks there. Our strategy, though, has been not to distort monetary policy in order to address those risks directly. Indeed, insufficient monetary policy accommodation, if it leads to a weaker economy and bad credit outcomes, and so on, is also a financial stability risk.

So our basic approach has been, at least for the first, second, and third lines of defense, to rely on supervision, regulation, monitoring macroprudential policies, and that whole set of tools that we have and are developing to try to avoid potential problems.

We also look very carefully at the implications of any potential kind of financial imbalance. For example, is that asset class heavily leveraged? Is it supported heavily by leverage, which would in turn mean that a sharp drop in that valuation would lead to other types of problems? Those are the kinds of things we look at, and we've greatly increased our ability to monitor and analyze those types of situations.

So our goal is to address financial instability concerns primarily, at least in the first instance, through supervision, regulation, and other microeconomic types of tools. But it is something that, of the various costs that have been ascribed to QE, is the only one that I find personally credible, frankly. And it's the one that we have spent the most time thinking about and trying to make sure that we can address as best we can.

AHAMED: Sort of bottom line for the moment: you're not worried about too much froth in financial markets?

BERNANKE: It's always bad luck to make any forecast about any particular market, but the markets currently seem to be broadly within the metrics of market valuation, and seem to be broadly within historical ranges. The financial system is strong. Key financial institutions are well capitalized, so we're watching this very vigilantly.

We've developed a tremendous additional capacity for doing that. But at this point, you know, we don't think that—and I think I can speak for my colleagues in this—we don't think that financial stability concerns should, at this point, detract from the need for monetary policy accommodation, which we are continuing to provide.

AHAMED: Has the crisis done long-lasting damage to the economy? And if so, what are the channels that you really worry about?

BERNANKE: That's an excellent question, and I don't think we'll know the answer for a while. First, it's important to say that there's been a benefit, which is that, obviously, we've done a root-and-branch reformation of the financial regulatory system and of financial markets that will provide greater stability, I hope, and more effective credit provision in the future. So there is at least that benefit, although, of course, it was a very expensive gain.

There are some ways in which the crisis could have effects on, if you will, the supply side of the economy, which means it might have a longer-term implication.

One, of course, is the effect of long-term unemployment on labor supply. Obviously there's been a decline in labor force participation, part of which is certainly due to ongoing trends that were in place before the crisis, but some of which might be due to the depth of the recession itself, and that could affect the available labor supply going forward and has very important direct effects on those who are unemployed and their families, so that's certainly a concern.

It is, by the way, a motivation for being aggressive with monetary policy to try to prevent those kinds of effects from taking hold.

Another kind of perhaps longer-lasting effect has to do with productivity gains. We've seen a very slow increase in productivity recently. We don't fully understand why. Some of it may just be low demand, for example. But it could be that the financial crisis has led to a slower pace of innovation, a slower pace of firm formation, less capital investment, which has led in turn to a less rapid pace of innovation.

There's interesting work—there's an economic historian named Alexander Field, who's written that the 1930s were actually a period of great innovation, but it didn't show up in the productivity statistics because with the economy and depression there weren't markets sufficient to make those innovations commercial. So something similar may have happened to some extent here.

Now all that being said, these are important effects, but none of them are truly permanent. I mean, eventually the economy will return to the growth path it was on prior to the crisis or something close to that. So these are long-lasting and very serious potential effects, but I don't think that they are truly permanent.

Bernanke then fielded questions from the audience.

EDWARD LAMONT [businessman/Connecticut politician]: Mr. Chairman, as a student of history, can you talk about the role of the president. During the Great Depression we had Franklin Roosevelt Fireside Chats, the explainer-in-chief making some sense and comfort out of the chaos. Did we have that in 2008? Because my sense is the American people—

Main Street, Wall Street—that there's still a great deal of confusion, and I think we're paying the consequences of it even today.

BERNANKE: It was a big challenge to explain what was going on, and, you know, at the Federal Reserve we tried to do it. We didn't always succeed, I'm sure. I give President Bush actually a lot of credit. He gave a lot of leeway to me and to Secretary Paulson to do what we thought was right. He supported us throughout the process. I remember him going on television and giving a speech about the TARP, which must have been very difficult for him, given his political predilections and the cost of that from the political side.

So it was difficult, it was difficult. Communication was a challenge throughout this whole process, but I wouldn't put it on the president or anyone else. I mean, all of us who were involved in the policymaking had a role and a responsibility to explain as best we could. When I came to the Fed, I was very interested in increasing the transparency of the Fed, although my motivations were primarily for making monetary policy more predictable and more accountable.

But as it turned out, transparency was very helpful in other dimensions as well. In particular, you know, I tried where I could to bring the story, not just to markets and to other economists, but to a more Main Street type of audience, on television or in town halls and things of that sort.

But it was very challenging, frankly, to do that. We obviously had other things to do as well. If you look around the world, there are populist reactions in most countries where there were serious financial crises, and that's probably not avoidable completely.

And what we have to do is, again, to explain what we did, why we did it, and try to win back the confidence of the public. And that's, I think, an important objective for all of us around the world.

GARRETT MITCHELL (*The Mitchell Report*): I'm interested in whether this experience has caused you to think in different terms about the strengths and weaknesses of our political system, and in particular how you think the system, and I mean that writ large—the executive branch, the Congress, the people themselves—whether it gave you a different perspective on how well American governance is working in the twenty-first century?

BERNANKE: There are two separate questions there. One has to do with sort of the structure of the American government as given to us by the Constitution and all of the evolution of the government since then. And then there's a question of our current political situation in terms of the mix of views and ideologies that are currently on the Hill, in particular.

In terms of the former, without making a judgment at all—and I'm certainly not qualified to make a judgment about overall political systems—one thing that really struck me during the crisis was that the governments that had more parliamentary-type systems were better able to respond quickly to a financial crisis.

It was envisioned in the Constitution that the president might have to act quickly to respond to a military or some kind of foreign relations crisis. That's why the president has a lot of flexibility to take action in the event of a military attack, for example—of course, ultimately going to Congress to get ratification.

During the crisis, the British, for example, very quickly put together a plan to address their banking problems because in this particular case they had a government that controlled the legislature and was able to respond quickly. So I think that turned out to be a problem [for us] during the crisis.

Now, obviously, some of the legislative actions that have been taken, Dodd-Frank and so on, have tried to set up frameworks whereby the Fed, the Treasury, and other regulators would be able to take necessary actions, like the liquidation authority. So there has been an attempt to address that structural problem with respect to financial crises.

On the broader question of governance, I have felt some frustration. Certainly it's been a concern that we've had these periods of fights over the debt limit and things of that sort. And I think those things have caused problems for the economy. They've hit confidence. They certainly have prevented more positive, constructive action on the part of the government to address some of these concerns in terms of unemployment, for example. But that's not a feature of the nature of our government. It's just the current situation in terms of the disagreements and range of views that are currently on the Hill.

KRISHNA GUHA (International Strategy & Investment Group): When we look beyond the legacy of the crisis itself in terms of deleveraging, there are other factors at play. The aging of the population here in the United States and in much of the industrialized world, the increasingly fractural distribution of income gains, as well as international factors such as the continuation of the global savings glut, reserve accumulation by emerging market economies. When you look over the longer sweep ahead beyond when we may have finally achieved full employment again, do you expect that we will be in an era of sustained low interest rates?

BERNANKE: I wasn't expecting that little end there to that question. Part of the implication of your question is the zero lower bound, is that going to be relevant a lot or not. It's hard to know.

Certainly there are a couple of ways of avoiding zero lower bound. One would be to avoid deep recessions like the one that we are now emerging from. Another would be to use a more balanced mix of monetary and fiscal policy when responding to recessions so as not to over-rely on low interest rate monetary policies.

Given inflation, the determinative long-run interest rates, it's going to be the rate of return to capital investment, productivity, and so on, and that's a huge debate, as you know. I guess that the jury is still out about longer-term technological trends and the productivity of capital.

One of the other things you mentioned has been part of the concern: the global savings glut. During the period before the crisis, the United States had a 6 percent trade deficit. We still have a trade deficit—which means, of course, that 6 percent of our domestic arch of demand is being drained off essentially abroad. At the same time, we, among the richest countries in the world, are receiving large amounts of capital inflows. Both of those things are going to tend to push down interest rates.

So one way to address low interest rate problems would be to get better balance in growth in terms of trade and capital flows. Another way, again, is to have a better balance of monetary and fiscal policy, including good investments in productivity-enhancing projects like effective infrastructure, for example.

But in the end it's going to depend a lot on the return to innovation, return to new capital. That question is still very much open, but I'm not yet ready to conclude that very low interest rates are going to be a permanent condition.

3

MONETARY POLICY WHEN RATES HIT ZERO
Putting Theory into Practice

JOHN C. WILLIAMS

It has been said, "An economist is a man who, when he finds something works in practice, wonders if it works in theory."[1] The study of the zero lower bound (ZLB) on nominal interest rates is an example of precisely the opposite: economists first figuring out what works in theory and then seeing if it works in practice. Japan's experience with price deflation and zero short-term interest rates beginning in the 1990s led to a flurry of economic research on the ZLB and its implications for monetary policy (see, for example, Benhabib, Schmitt-Grohé, and Uribe 2001; Eggertsson and Woodford 2003; Reifschneider and Williams 2000; and references therein). This research came to a number of concrete conclusions and policy prescriptions that influenced policymaking during and after the global financial crisis.

The opinions expressed in this paper are those of the author and do not necessarily reflect the views of any other individuals within the Federal Reserve System. I thank Early Elias and Kuni Natsuki for excellent research assistance, and Eric Swanson for assistance in compiling research results.
    1. This quotation is often attributed to the economist Walter Heller.

One conclusion from the precrisis research was that the ZLB was a problem that could potentially afflict any economy with a sufficiently low inflation target, but that the episodes at the ZLB would be relatively infrequent and generally short-lived. For example, Reifschneider and Williams (2000) found that under a standard Taylor (1993) monetary policy rule and a 2 percent inflation target, monetary policy would be constrained at the ZLB about 5 percent of the time, and ZLB episodes would typically last just one year. Other research came to even more sanguine conclusions regarding the likely effects of the ZLB, in part because that research was often predicated on an economic environment similar to the tranquil Great Moderation period of the 1980s and 1990s in the United States (see, for example, Adam and Billi 2006; Coenen, Orphanides, and Wieland 2004; Schmitt-Grohé and Uribe 2007).

Second, this research identified monetary policy strategies that should be effective at reducing most of the adverse effects of the ZLB. Specifically, short-term rates should be cut aggressively when deflation or a severe downturn threatens (Reifschneider and Williams 2000, 2002). That is, do *not* "keep your powder dry." In addition, short-term rates should be kept "lower for longer" as the economy recovers (Eggertson and Woodford 2003; Reifschneider and Williams 2000, 2002). In theory, the expectation of a sustained low level of short-term interest rates reduces longer-term yields and eases financial conditions more broadly. In these two ways, the maximal amount of monetary stimulus can be put into place quickly. Indeed, this research found that such strategies should, in most cases, be sufficient to nearly fully offset the effects of the ZLB on the economy.

Third, some researchers argued that unconventional policy actions such as central bank large-scale asset purchases (LSAP) of longer-term securities or foreign exchange can complement conventional policy actions by making financial conditions more favorable for growth even when short rates are constrained by the ZLB (Bernanke and Reinhart 2004; Bernanke, Reinhart, and Sack 2004; McCallum 2000; Svensson 2001).

Of course, within a few years of the publication of this research, the ZLB went from being a theoretical concern to a very real practical problem for many central banks across the globe. Figure 3-1 shows the policy rates for four major advanced economies since 1990. The Bank of England, the Bank of Japan, the European Central Bank, and the Federal

FIGURE 3-1. The ZLB: Not Just an Academic Concern

Short-term interest rates (percent)

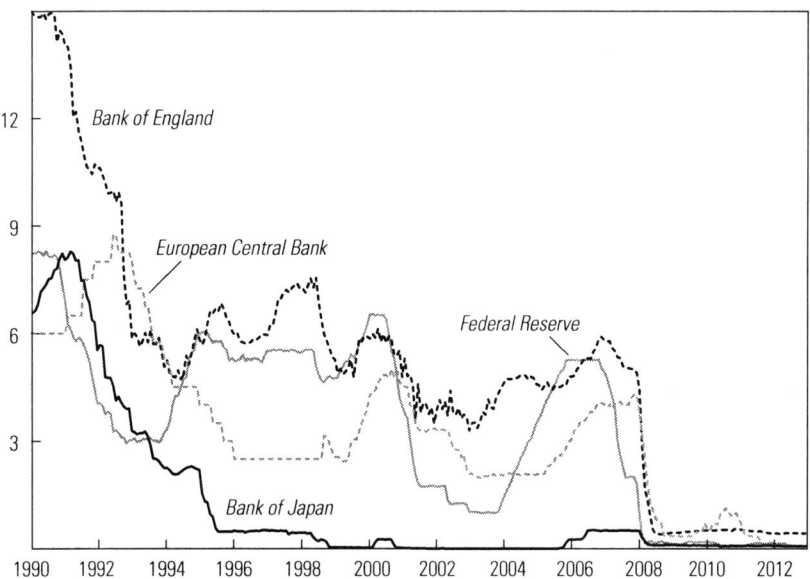

Sources: Board of Governors of the Federal Reserve System (2013); Organization for Economic Cooperation and Development (OECD, 2013).

Reserve all brought their policy rates to their respective effective lower bounds in late 2008 or early 2009. Central banks quickly sought to put into practice many of the prescriptions that researchers had identified.

The experiences of the past six years provide a wealth of data on what works and what doesn't, which theories have proved useful, and which need to be reconsidered. This essay reexamines the three key issues just outlined, all highlighted in research related to the ZLB, and lays out three still unanswered questions for monetary policy in a world where the ZLB is an ongoing concern.

HISTORY MATTERS:
REASSESSING THE RISK OF THE ZERO LOWER BOUND

The events of the past six years have called into question some of the assumptions in previous research that found that episodes of hitting the ZLB would likely be relatively infrequent and short-lived. Chung and his colleagues (2012) show that a wide range of modern macroeconomic forecasting models based on postwar U.S. data predict that the probability of recent events, including multiple years stuck at the ZLB, is extremely remote—essentially nonexistent. The overwhelming falsification of this prediction can be interpreted in one of two ways. Either recent events represent an extraordinary run of horribly bad luck—a 100-year flood, if you will—or the models are badly misspecified, in particular with regard to their implications for negative tail risk.

Given the limited real-world empirical evidence on the frequency and severity of ZLB episodes, researchers have had to rely on artificial data generated by stochastic simulations of macroeconomic models to infer these probabilities and effects. Although the results depend on the details of the model specification and other assumptions, two key factors affect the simulated probability of hitting the ZLB and the resulting effects of the ZLB on the macroeconomy: (1) the size and (2) the duration of the shocks hitting the economy. If the shocks are assumed to be typically small, then the monetary policy response will be correspondingly small and the ZLB will rarely come into play. Similarly, if the shocks are assumed to be transitory, episodes of the ZLB will also tend to be short and will have relatively modest effects on the economy.

The standard approach in the research literature has been to estimate the shock processes on the basis of historical data. They key issue is this: what data should one use? The lack of consistent time series of data covering a very long period and a concern that structural change has made data from long ago no longer relevant caused most researchers to focus on evidence on macroeconomic disturbances from the past twenty-five to fifty years. The advantage of this approach is that it provides consistent, reasonably accurate data for analysis. The downside to relying on data from recent decades is that a relatively small sample can provide a misleading view of the frequency of tail events. This is particularly true for the unusually tranquil quarter century before the recent global financial crisis, which contributed to a false sense that the business cycle had been tamed.

How can we avoid overreliance on short samples in evaluating tail risks while basing our analysis on the empirical evidence? One alternative approach that is arguably more robust to overconfidence based on small samples is to look at much broader historical experience across a

FIGURE 3-2. History Matters a Lot

Observations falling in the indicated range

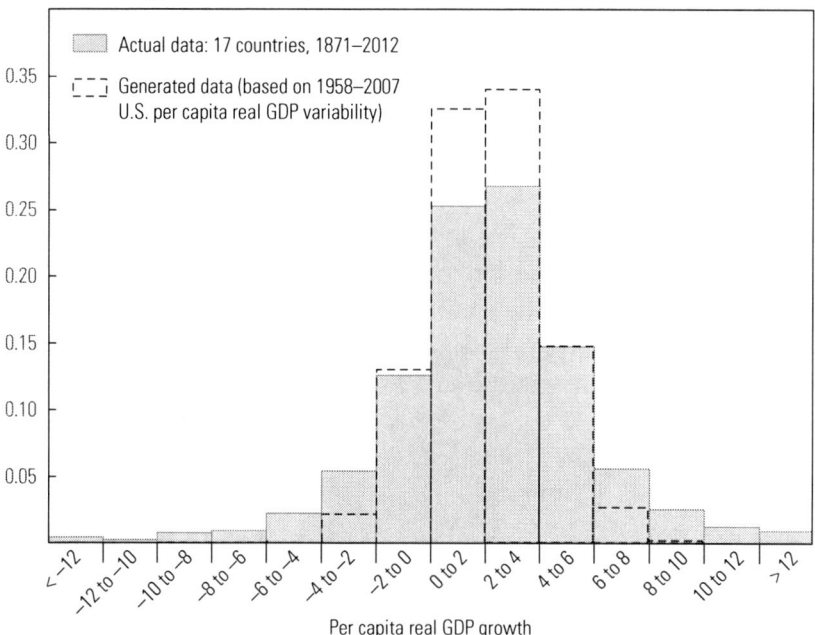

Per capita real GDP growth

Source: Barro and Ursúa (2010), updated by the author.

wide range of economies. This approach explicitly rejects the "this time is different" view that downplays old or distant events, and instead treats a wide range of historical experience as potentially informative in describing the types of risks that the future may hold.

Figure 3-2 illustrates that a broader historical perspective can paint a picture that is very different from the postwar U.S. data. The gray bars show the distribution of annual per capita real GDP growth from a sample of seventeen advanced countries over the period 1871–2012, excluding years of major wars.[2] The x-axis indicates ranges for annual

2. Following Jordà, Schularick, and Taylor (2011), the data are taken from Barro and Ursúa (2010), and updated for 2007–12 using data from the World Bank (2013). For the United States, data for 1930–2012 are the current national income and product data from the Bureau of Economic Analysis. The countries in the sample are Australia, Belgium, Canada, Denmark, Finland, France, Germany, Great Britain, Italy, Japan, Netherlands, Norway, Portugal, Spain, Sweden, Switzerland, and the United States.

per capita real GDP growth (measured in log differences). The y-axis shows the share of observations from the sample where the observed data lie in the indicated range. I am not arguing that we should blithely base conclusions on this particular dataset, but rather that we use it to illustrate the broader point that a larger sample may provide insights into tail events that small samples miss.

One aspect of the broad historical data stands out: sharp declines in economic activity occur relatively frequently. To put this in perspective, per capita real U.S. GDP fell by 3.7 percent in 2009. In the broad historical experience represented by these seventeen countries, a decline of that magnitude or larger occurs 5.2 percent of the time—that is, about once every nineteen years on average. Even if one abstracts from the experiences of the other countries and looks only at the U.S. data from 1871 to 2012, a decline of this magnitude occurs in 7.8 percent of the sample years, or about once every thirteen years. On the basis of these metrics, recent events would scarcely be considered rare or unprecedented. Instead, history teaches that very large downturns are not only possible—they are probable.

Interestingly, these large declines in output do not represent extreme tail events relative to the rest of the distribution. If one takes the mean and variance of the observations from the broad historical sample, the normal distribution implies a probability of declines of 3.7 percent or greater in 8.2 percent of the time, somewhat higher than the observed rate of 5.2 percent. Thus one does not need to resort to arguments about fat-tailed distributions to understand the data: it suffices to allow for a sufficiently large variance.

A very different perspective on the likelihood of recent events emerges if one instead looks exclusively at the postwar U.S. experience. In the fifty years before the crisis, there was no year in which U.S. per capita real GDP fell by more than 3 percent. Given the dearth of extreme tail events, one is forced to construct a theoretical probability based on the available data. The dashed lines in figure 3-2 illustrate one such attempt. The dashed lines show the histogram for a hypothetical economy with the same sample mean growth rate as the long sample of seventeen countries, but with the variance of the growth rate set equal to that observed in the U.S. data over the period 1958–2007. The distribution of outcomes is assumed to be normally and independently distributed.

This distribution illustrates the types of assumption regarding macro-economic variability typically used in past research on the ZLB.

The experience of the postwar period suggests the probability of experiencing a year as bad as 2008 is exceedingly low. Using the variance in the U.S. data over the fifty years before the crisis, one would expect a downturn as bad as occurred in 2008 less than one-quarter of 1 percent of the time, or about once every 430 years. The corresponding figure based on variance in the data during the Great Moderation period is essentially zero, at 0.003 percent, or once every 33,000 years! These overoptimistic predictions are due to the historically low variance in per capita real output growth during the decades before the crisis. The numbers tell the story. The standard deviation of the U.S. per capita GDP growth from 1958 through 2007 is 2.1 percentage points, half that of the broad historical data (4.2 percentage points). The difference is even greater if one looks at data from the Great Moderation period: the standard deviation of per capita real GDP growth over the period 1983–2007 is a mere 1.45 percentage points, about one-third that of the broad historical experience. The miniscule implied probabilities of a severe downturn simply reflect the predicted rarity of approximately three and four standard deviation tail events.

In addition to the size of the shocks, the duration of shocks matters for considering the repercussions of the ZLB. Macroeconomic models typically build in a great deal of correction to the mean, consistent with the behavior of postwar U.S. data. This contrasts with a key lesson from history that banking and financial crises are often followed by slow recoveries (Jordà, Schularick, and Taylor 2011; Reinhart and Rogoff 2009). As a result, standard models systematically underpredict the length of ZLB episodes.

One approach to duration of shocks is to examine multiyear declines in output. Consider the two-year decline in output during the recent financial crisis, when per capita real GDP fell by about 5 percent over the period 2008–09. In the broad historical experience represented by the seventeen countries, a two-year decline of that magnitude or larger occurs 4.4 percent of the time, that is, about once every twenty-three years on average—not a common occurrence, but also not unheard of. From the variance in the U.S. data over the fifty years before the crisis, one would expect a two-year downturn of that magnitude once every

FIGURE 3-3. The Duration of Macroeconomic Shocks

Estimates of the natural rate of interest (percent)

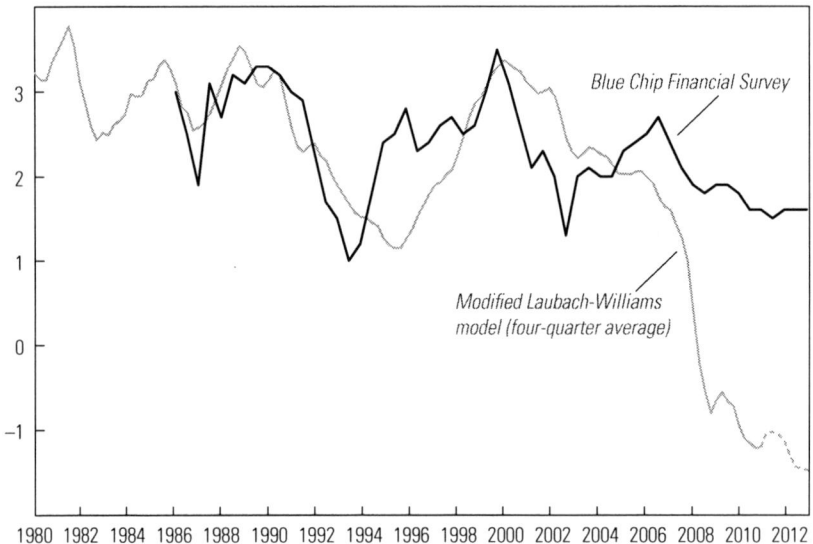

Source: Blue Chip Financial Survey (2013); Laubach and Williams (2003), modified by the author.

570 years. Once again, if one focuses on the Great Moderation period, the probability of such an outcome is virtually nonexistent, occurring on average about once every 6,800 years.

One does not need to look at distant history to see the effects of highly persistent shocks on the economy. A useful summary statistic for the extent of such shocks is the natural rate of interest, which measures the real interest rate consistent with the economy being at equilibrium. A number of factors—including persistent changes in productivity growth, preferences, and fiscal policy—affect the natural rate of interest over time. Laubach and Williams (2003) develop a model that estimates the medium-term natural rate of interest for the United States. Figure 3-3 shows estimates of the medium-term natural rate of interest from a version of this model.[3] For comparison, the figure also shows the medium-

3. The model-based estimate is from a modified version of the Laubach and Williams (2003) model. The modification is that the average of gross domestic product and gross domestic income is used as the output measure in the model, instead of gross domestic product as in the original.

term forecasts of the real federal funds rate from the Blue Chip Financial Survey (2013) of economic forecasters.

Both the model-based and survey-based estimates of the medium-term natural rate of interest show significant variation over time. In particular, those estimates indicate persistent declines following the savings and loan crisis of the late 1980s and since the onset of the global financial crisis, reflecting the persistent headwinds to economic growth that typically follow banking and financial crises.

In summary, when viewed through the lens of the postwar U.S. experience, the depth and duration of the recent recession may appear extraordinary. However, a broader look at economic history and events around the world demonstrates that deep and long-lasting downturns are not that rare.

CONVENTIONAL MONETARY POLICY AND THE ZERO LOWER BOUND

As noted in the preceding section, the research on conventional monetary policy in the vicinity of the ZLB has yielded two strong policy prescriptions. First, policymakers should act aggressively in cutting rates to maximize the monetary stimulus when deflation or a sharp decline in output threatens. Second, monetary policy should remain more accommodative than implied by standard policy prescriptions after a period when the ZLB constrains policy. This is often referred to as a "lower for longer" strategy. The logic behind this approach is to lower future expected interest rates and thereby boost spending immediately, thereby reducing the lost output resulting from the shock and avoiding disinflation. Moreover, in theory it can be advantageous to lower interest rate expectations to the point that inflation is expected to rise above the target for some time, thereby lowering real interest rates and further reducing lost output.

As the crisis emerged, major central banks followed the first prescription, aggressively cutting rates (figure 3-1). All four major central banks brought their policy rates to their effective lower bounds by early 2009. Other central banks in advanced economies—including Australia, Canada, Israel, New Zealand, Norway, and Sweden—also brought rates down quickly as the global financial crisis unfolded.

The prescription of lower for longer was less actively employed during the recession and early stages of the recovery. In the United States, the Federal Open Market Committee (FOMC) communicated a general expectation of low rates in the future. For example, in its December 2008 statement the FOMC stated that it expected to keep the funds rate low "for some time" (Board of Governors of the Federal Reserve System 2008). This represented a throwback to the qualitative forward guidance used by the FOMC in 2003 and 2004. (For a detailed discussion of this earlier episode, see Rudebusch and Williams 2008.)

Despite this qualitative forward guidance, the public held the view that a policy tightening was just around the corner. From the beginning of 2009 to mid-2011, expectations from financial markets and surveys of economists consistently showed the federal funds rate lifting off from the zero bound within a year or so. The bold line at the extreme left of figure 3-4 shows the evolution of Blue Chip consensus real-time forecasts from January 2009 through August 2011 for the date of the funds rate liftoff from its 0–25 basis point range that was instituted in December 2008. The x-axis indicates the date the forecast was published. The y-axis indicates the date at which forecasters predicted the FOMC would raise the funds rate for the first time. For example, in the first half of 2011 the consensus forecast in the Blue Chip Financial Survey was for liftoff in the second quarter of 2012. Note that the Blue Chip Financial Survey forecast horizon is typically limited to seven quarters. The dot in figure 3-4 corresponds to the September 2011 survey. It indicates that liftoff was not expected to occur within the reported forecast horizon (which ended in the second quarter of 2013 for that survey). This remained true until the Blue Chip Financial Survey started explicitly asking about the timing of liftoff in early 2013; the results from these questions are shown in the short bold line segment at the extreme right in figure 3-4.

What is striking about this early period is the public's conviction that the Federal Reserve would quickly raise rates again. This belief persisted despite the efforts of many on the FOMC to communicate the severity of the downturn and the resulting need for highly accommodative monetary policy for quite some time. Evidently, the public simply did not know what to expect given that short-term rates were at zero and policymakers couldn't shift expectations simply by cutting rates

FIGURE 3-4. Expectations of Federal Reserve Funds Rate Liftoff

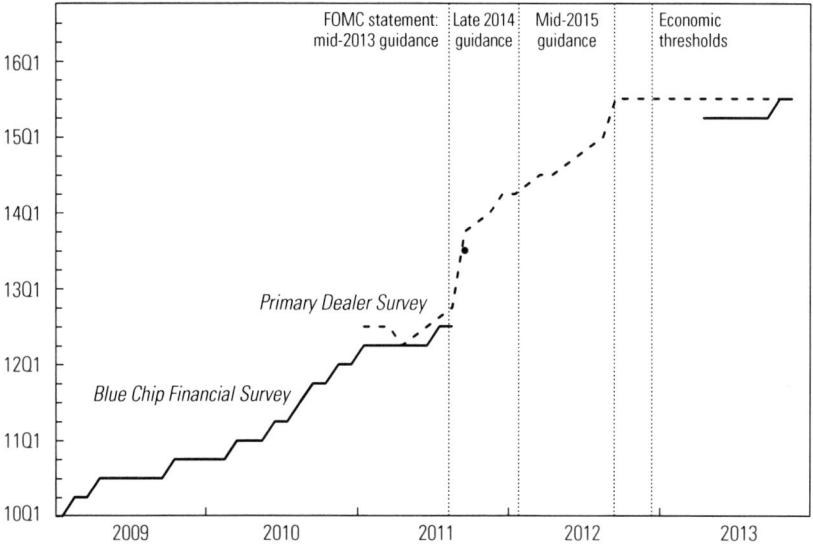

Expected liftoff date

Source: Blue Chip Financial Survey (2013); Federal Reserve Bank of New York (2013).

further.[4] The same pattern is seen in the U.K. forecast data (Swanson and Williams 2013).

To push back against these excessively tight expectations, the FOMC made its forward guidance more explicit and forceful. In August 2011 it announced that economic conditions were "likely to warrant exceptionally low levels for the federal funds rate at least through mid-2013" (Board of Governors of the Federal Reserve 2011). In so doing, the FOMC mimicked the approach taken earlier by the Bank of Canada in April 2009, which proved effective at modestly shifting interest rate expectations (Carney 2012).

The FOMC's August 2011 announcement had a dramatic effect on financial market expectations. It caused an immediate 10 basis-point drop in two-year Treasury yields and a greater than 20 basis-point decline in longer-term yields. This shift in policy expectations is also

4. For further discussion of the problem of expectations formation at the ZLB, see Reifschneider and Roberts (2006) and Williams (2006).

evident in market expectations of the future path for the funds rate, shown in figure 3-4. Before the August FOMC announcement, the Blue Chip consensus was that the FOMC would raise rates in the third quarter of 2012. In the survey following the announcement, expectations in the Blue Chip forecast were for no rate increase over the next seven quarters (the limit of the forecast horizon). Similarly, the Federal Reserve Bank of New York's survey of primary dealers shows the expected time of liftoff from the zero bound jumping from late 2012 to late 2013 following the FOMC's August 2011 announcement.[5] The FOMC's quantitative forward guidance was extended further in January 2012 to "late 2014" and again in September 2012 to "mid-2015," also with significant effects on policy expectations and yields. Directly following these announcements, longer-term rates fell by between 3 and 9 basis points. As seen in figure 3-4, the primary dealer survey shows expectations of funds rate liftoff being pushed out farther during 2012 in line with FOMC communications. In addition, in January 2012 the FOMC started publishing its projections of the federal funds rate for the next few years (along with those for GDP unemployment and inflation), providing further information on the likely future path of short-term interest rates. The FOMC policy projections should help the public understand the Federal Reserve's reaction function—that is, how policy changes as economic conditions evolve (Rudebusch and Williams 2008).

In December 2012 the FOMC replaced the date-based guidance with language that explicitly ties its forward guidance to the state of the economy. The FOMC stated it was likely to keep the funds rate near zero, "at least as long as the unemployment rate remains above 6 1/2 percent" (Board of Governors of the Federal Reserve System 2012) and as long as inflation is not expected to exceed 2.5 percent over the next year or two an inflation expectations remain anchored. In December 2013 the FOMC statement language was modified to indicate that liftoff was likely to occur well after the time when the unemployment rate falls below 6 1/2 percent. This state-based forward guidance is still a relatively new experiment in FOMC transparency, but it has already proven to be an effective communication tool, focusing public attention

---

5. For analysis of the effects of FOMC communications on market expectations, see Femia, Friedman, and Sack (2013).

on economic milestones in contemplating future policy decisions. Subsequent to the Federal Reserve's use of state-based policy guidance, the Bank of England has followed suit in its policy communications.

Beyond the shifts in policy expectations following these announcements, the introduction of explicit forward guidance has fundamentally changed the behavior of public expectations of future interest rates. This can be seen in the Treasury market reaction to economic news that normally would cause medium-term interest rates to change in anticipation of monetary policy responses. In examining how market reactions to news have changed since the federal funds rate has fallen to almost zero, Swanson and Williams (2012) note that from January 2009 through August 2011, one-year Treasury yields responded about half as much as they responded in times when short-term interest rates were not close to zero. Since the introduction of explicit forward guidance in August 2011, one-year yields have responded one-tenth as much as usual. The shift in expectations of interest rates out two years is even more dramatic: from January 2009 to August 2011, responsiveness to news was only slightly muted, at about 85 percent of the usual response. Following the August announcement, responsiveness fell to one-quarter as much as usual. Swanson and Williams see a similar pattern in the expectations of future short-term interest rates as measured by the responsiveness of Eurodollar futures to economic news. This evidence demonstrates that explicit forward guidance can effectively anchor interest rate expectations out two years.

An international comparison is illuminating regarding the effects of quantitative forward guidance. As already mentioned, the Bank of Canada was an early adopter, but Canada's spell at the ZLB lasted only a year. In the United Kingdom, forward guidance was introduced only recently. Until the summer of 2011, forecasters expected the Bank of England to raise interest rates within a few quarters. Interestingly, expectations shifted dramatically around the same time as they did in the United States. The same shift in expectations is in evidence in a sharp decline in the responsiveness of one- and two-year gilt yields since the summer of 2011 (Swanson and Williams 2013). Despite the lack of quantitative forward guidance, interest rate expectations in the United Kingdom appear to be very well anchored.

The euro area provides a stark contrast. One- and two-year German bund yields showed no significant decline in responsiveness to news until 2012, suggesting that market participants viewed the European Central Bank (ECB) as being on the cusp of changing rates during that period (Swanson and Williams 2013). That perception was likely reinforced when the ECB increased the main refinancing rate in 2011. Interestingly, the responsiveness of these yields fell to close to zero in 2012, similar to the experience in the United States and United Kingdom, possibly reflecting the change in the tone of communication from the ECB regarding monetary policy.

Overall, consistent with the prescription of research, central banks acted to cut rates very aggressively during the financial crisis. It took longer to effectively manage policy expectations. In the end, quantitative forward guidance proved highly effective at anchoring interest rate expectations consistent with policymakers' intentions.

INTO THE GREAT UNKNOWN: LARGE-SCALE ASSET PURCHASES

In standard textbook theory based on frictionless financial markets and the absence of arbitrage, large-scale asset purchases by central banks should have no effect on asset prices or the broader economy, all else equal. According to this theory, the price of an asset depends solely on its expected future returns, adjusted for risk. Since asset purchases by the central bank don't fundamentally change the risk-adjusted returns to assets, they should have no direct effect on asset prices or the economy.

Running against the grain of this conventional wisdom, a number of economists studied the potential role of alternative policy instruments—including expanding the central bank balance sheet by purchasing foreign and domestic sovereign debt—when the short-term interest rate was constrained by the ZLB. They focused on two potential ways such alternative policy instruments could affect the economy: (1) a signaling channel and (2) a preferred habitat channel.

According to the signaling channel, central bank asset purchases provide an indirect signal of the central bank's objectives and future conventional policy actions. This approach maintains the assumption of frictionless financial markets, so asset purchases on their own have no direct effect on financial conditions, economic activity, or inflation. Instead, they work solely by affecting public expectations of future short-term interest rates. For example, Svensson's (2001) recommendation to target an exchange rate works in his model because it anchors the price level and thereby promises earlier policy in the future needed to generate higher inflation following a ZLB episode. The proposals of targeting money supply or longer-term Treasury yields by Auerbach and Obstfeld (2005) and McGough, Rudebusch, and Williams (2005), respectively, can be interpreted similarly.

The second hypothesized channel abandons the frictionless financial market assumption and posits a direct effect of central bank purchases on asset prices. McCallum (2000), Coenen and Wieland (2004), and Bernanke, Reinhart, and Sack (2004) are pre-crisis examples of research based on this approach. The basic insight underlying this approach dates to mid-twentieth-century Nobel laureates Franco Modigliani and James Tobin, who argued that certain financial markets are segmented. (For a modern treatment, see Vayanos and Vila 2009.) Some investors, such as pension funds, have strong preferences or even legal restrictions on where they put their money. Such so-called preferred habitats for certain types of investments can interfere with the equalization of risk-adjusted returns to different assets. As a result, the relative supply and demand of assets, which are imperfect substitutes for each other, affects their prices.

Before the crisis, almost everything known about the effects of large-scale asset purchases came from studies of the Japanese lost decade and a few scattered episodes in the United States, such as Operation Twist in the 1960s and changes in the demand or supply of Treasury securities (Bernanke, Reinhart, and Sack 2004; Modigliani and Sutch 1966, 1967). That void was filled once the Federal Reserve and other central banks introduced large-scale asset purchase programs and economists were able to carefully study their effects.[6] Table 3-1 summarizes the results from a large number of research papers that differ in methodology and data.[7]

Two themes emerge from this research on the effects of asset purchases on asset prices. First, although individual estimates differ, this

6. In addition, in September 2011 the Swiss National Bank announced a floor on the euro–Swiss franc exchange rate of 1.2, which they have subsequently defended through foreign exchange operations.

7. See the sources in table 3-1.

TABLE 3-1. Estimates of LSAP Effects on Longer-Term Interest Rates

Study	Sample	Method	Representative estimates of effect of $600 billion LSAP (±2 std errors if avail.)
Modigliani-Sutch (1966, 1967)	Operation Twist	time series	0 bp (±20 bp)
Bernanke-Reinhart-Sack (2004)	Japan, United States	event study	400 bp (±370 bp), 40 bp (±60 bp)
Greenwood-Vayanos (2008)	postwar United States (precrisis)	time series	14 bp (±7 bp)
Krishnamurthy–Vissing-Jorgensen (2011, 2012)	postwar U.S., LSAP1, and LSAP2	time series	15 bp (±5 bp)
Gagnon-Raskin-Remache-Sack (2011)	LSAP1	event study, time series	30 bp (±15 bp), 18 bp (±7 bp)
D'Amico-King (2013)	LSAP1 Treasury purchases	security-specific event study	100 bp (±80 bp)
Hamilton-Wu (2011)	U.S., 1990–LSAP2	affine no-arbitrage model	17 bp
Hancock-Passmore (2011)	LSAP1 MBS purchases	time series	30 bp
Swanson (2011)	Operation Twist	event study	15 bp (±10 bp)
Joyce-Lasaosa-Stevens-Tong (2011)	U.K. LSAPs	event study, time series	40 bp
Neely (2013)	effect of U.S. LSAP1 on foreign bond yields	event study	17 bp (±13 bp)
Christensen-Rudebusch (2012)	LSAP1, LSAP2, and U.K. LSAPs	event study, affine no-arbitrage model	10 bp
D'Amico et al. (2012)	United States, precrisis	weekly time series	45 bp
Bauer-Rudebusch (forthcoming)	LSAP1, LSAP2	event study, affine no-arbitrage model	16 bp
Li-Wei (2013)	United States, precrisis	affine no-arbitrage model	26 bp

Note: bp = basis point; LSAP1, LSAP2, etc. = large-scale asset purchase (LSAP) program 1, 2, etc.; MBS = mortgage-backed securities.

analysis consistently finds that asset purchases have sizable effects on yields on longer-term securities. Second, there remains a great deal of uncertainty about the magnitude of these effects and their impact on the overall economy.

The central tendency of the estimates reported in table 3-1 indicates that $600 billion of the Federal Reserve's asset purchases lowers the yield on ten-year Treasury notes by around 15 to 25 basis points. To put that in perspective, that is roughly the same size move in longer-term yields one would expect from a cut in the federal funds rate of 3/4 to 1 percentage point (Chung and others 2012; Gürkaynak, Sack, and Swanson 2005, table 5).

A recent case study shows how changes in expectations of the Federal Reserve's asset purchases affect longer-term interest rates and financial conditions more broadly. After the FOMC's announcement on September 18 that it would not change the pace of asset purchases, the yield on the ten-year Treasury note fell by 18 basis points.[8] The effects didn't stop there. The stock market rose about 1.25 percent and the value of the dollar against the euro fell by around 1 percent.

Although research consistently finds sizable effects on asset purchases on longer-term yields, there is a great deal of uncertainty about the magnitude of these effects and the impact on the economy. For estimates for which we have estimated standard errors, the figures are generally not very precise, with associated *t*-statistics often equal to or less than two. In addition, looking across the studies, the estimated effects vary considerably. For example, if one drops the two highest and two lowest estimates in table 3-1, the remaining thirteen range from 14 to 45 basis points.

Although the literature provides information on the magnitude of the effects of asset purchases, it is still unclear to what extent these effects are due to the signaling or preferred habitat channels. Krishnamurthy and Vissing-Jorgensen (2011, 2012) find incomplete pass-through from asset purchases to prices of other securities. Because the signaling channel implies a broad effect across securities, this provides indirect evidence in favor of a role for the preferred habitat view that some assets are imperfect substitutes for others. Bauer and Rudebusch (forthcoming) find that it is very difficult to disentangle the effects from the two channels, but conclude that the preponderance of evidence suggests both channels play a significant role in the United States. In contrast, Christensen and Rudebusch (2012) find that asset purchases in the United Kingdom had little signaling effect and worked primarily through the preferred habitat channel.

---

8. See Federal Open Market Committee, September 18, 2013, announcement at http://www.federalreserve.gov/newsevents/press/monetary/20130918a.htm.

Estimating the effects of large-scale asset purchases on the economy—as opposed to financial markets—is inherently much harder to do and is subject to greater uncertainty. The effects of lower longer-term interest rates take place over the course of many months and even years; over those longer horizons it is hard to know how much of the change in economic activity was due to the effects of monetary policy or other factors. In addition, standard macroeconomic models assume frictionless financial markets and therefore do not allow for imperfect substitutability of assets. Theories about the effects of movements in asset prices caused by changes in relative supply and demand are still in their infancy.[9] Until these models are more fully developed, one must make do with the models at hand, appropriately modified to incorporate asset purchases.

In one such study, Chung and his colleagues (2012) use the Federal Reserve Board's large-scale macroeconomic model to estimate the effects of the Federal Reserve's $600 billion large-scale asset purchase initiated in 2011 (often referred to as QE2). They find that the program lowered the unemployment rate by about 1/4 percentage point. This model assumes that changes in Treasury yields due to the asset purchase program fully spill over to other asset prices, and that private spending depends directly on these asset prices. For comparison, Chen, Cúrdia, and Ferrero (2012) (building on the model of Andrés, López-Salido, and Nelson 2004) stipulate segmented markets for ownership of different types of assets. They find asset purchases to have smaller effects on the economy. Despite these differences, both analyses find that asset purchases are most effective at stimulating the economy when they work in concert with expectations of sustained easy conventional monetary policy.

Even for a given model, the estimated effects of asset purchases on the economy are subject to considerable uncertainty. One estimate is that the degree of uncertainty regarding the macroeconomic effects of asset purchases is at least twice as large as that for conventional monetary policy (Williams 2013a). Although researchers have made great strides in measuring the effects of these policies on financial conditions,

---

9. For a discussion of the issues and one approach to modeling the effects of asset purchases on the economy, see Araújo, Schommer, and Woodford (2013).

considerably more research is needed into their effects on the real economy and inflation.

UNRESOLVED ISSUES

The experience of the past six years has demonstrated the valuable contributions of economic theory and research in thinking through abstract economic issues before they became reality. It has also provided a store of new information regarding the incidence and consequences of the ZLB. In particular, we have learned that the ZLB is a serious practical issue that is very likely to constrain policy in the future, and that there are implementable policy actions that can help offset some, if not all, of the ZLB's deleterious effects.

Looking ahead, there remain a number of key unresolved issues related to the ZLB. Three come immediately to mind. First, should central banks change their policy frameworks from inflation targeting to one of price-level or nominal-GDP targeting in order to better anchor expectations of future policy actions? One lesson from the recent past is the difficulty in anchoring policy expectations when the short rate is at the ZLB. Although quantitative forward guidance has proven a useful tool, it suffers from a number of limitations. Experience has shown that it is impossible to convey the full reach of factors that influence the future course of policy. As a result, forward guidance ends up being oversimplified and prone to misinterpretation. Moreover, forward guidance several years in advance may not be credible, especially in light of the change in policymakers over time. In theory, alternative frameworks such as nominal-GDP targeting, if fully understood by the public, could help resolve these communication difficulties (Williams 2006; Woodford 2013), but at some potential cost.

Second, should large-scale asset purchases be a standard tool of monetary policy at the ZLB, and, if so, how should they be implemented? As just mentioned, asset purchases have proven a potent but blunt tool, with uncertain effects on financial markets and the economy. In addition, there are nagging concerns that large-scale asset purchases carry with them particular risks to the economy or the health of the financial system that we still don't understand well. Although most central banks used a quantity-based approach to implementing asset purchases, the Swiss National Bank used a price-based approach. These are issues that require further study and analysis.

Finally, and most controversially, in light of the experience of the costs of the ZLB and central banks' abilities to counter them, does the 2 percent inflation target adopted by many central banks provide a sufficient cushion to allow monetary policy to successfully stabilize the economy and inflation in the future?[10] On one side of the ledger, recent experience proves that the ZLB is a worse problem than previously imagined; consideration of the implications of the ZLB in the future will need to take this into account. On the other side, forward guidance, large-scale asset purchases, and, in some cases, fiscal policy have proven to be effective partial antidotes for the ZLB. Even if one views the risks from the ZLB to be greater than before, there are alternatives to raising the inflation target. More effective financial regulation may diminish the potential for a severe crisis for the foreseeable future. And, as I have also pointed out, adoption of a price-level or nominal-GDP targeting regime could potentially further reduce the costs of the ZLB. What is needed now, like the surge in research on the ZLB in the decade before the crisis, is a new flurry of studies on these issues that take into account the lessons of the past six years and help provide concrete prescriptions for future policymakers.

REFERENCES

Adam, Klaus, and Roberto M. Billi. 2006. "Optimal Monetary Policy under Commitment with a Zero Bound on Nominal Interest Rates." *Journal of Money, Credit and Banking* 38, no. 7: 1877–1905.

Andrés, Javier, David López-Salido, and Edward Nelson. 2004. "Tobin's Imperfect Assets Substitution in Optimizing General Equilibrium." *Journal of Money, Credit, and Banking* 36 (August):. 665–90.

Araújo, Aloísio, Susan Schommer, and Michael Woodford. 2013. "Conventional and Unconventional Monetary Policy with Endogenous Collateral Constraints." Paper presented at National Bureau of Economic Research Conference, Lessons from the Financial Crisis for Monetary Policy, October (http://conference.nber.org/confer/2013/FCMPf13/woodford_conference_submit.pdf).

---

10. See Blanchard, Dell'Ariccia, and Mauro (2010); Reifschneider and Williams (2000); Williams (2009).

Auerbach, Alan J., and Maurice Obstfeld. 2005. "The Case for Open-Market Purchases in a Liquidity Trap." *American Economic Review* 95, no. 1: 100–37.

Barro, Robert J., and José F. Ursúa. 2010. Macroeconomic Data (http://scholar.harvard.edu/barro/publications/barro-ursua-macroeconomic-data).

Bauer, Michael, and Glenn Rudebusch. Forthcoming. "The Signaling Channel for Federal Reserve Bond Purchases." *International Journal of Central Banking.*

Benhabib, Jess, Stephanie Schmitt-Grohé, and Martín Uribe. 2001. "The Perils of Taylor Rules." *Journal of Economic Theory* 96 (January): 40–69.

Bernanke, Ben S., and Vincent R. Reinhart. 2004. "Conducting Monetary Policy at Very Low Short-Term Interest Rates." *American Economic Review, Papers and Proceedings* 94 (May): 85–90.

Bernanke, Ben S., Vincent R. Reinhart, and Brian P. Sack. 2004. "Monetary Policy Alternatives at the Zero Bound: An Empirical Assessment." *Brookings Papers on Economic Activity*, pp. 1–78.

Blanchard, Olivier, Giovanni Dell'Ariccia, and Paolo Mauro. 2010. "Rethinking Macroeconomic Policy." International Monetary Fund Staff Position Note (February 12).

Blue Chip Financial Survey. Various years. New York: Aspen.

Board of Governors of the Federal Reserve System. 2008. Federal Reserve Press Release (FOMC Statement), December 16 (www.federalreserve.gov/newsevents/press/monetary/20081216b.htm).

———. 2011. Federal Reserve Press Release (FOMC Statement), August 9 (www.federalreserve.gov/newsevents/press/monetary/20110809a.htm).

———. 2012. Federal Reserve Press Release (FOMC Statement), December 12 (www.federalreserve.gov/newsevents/press/monetary/20121212a.htm).

———. 2013. Federal Reserve Statistical Release H.15. Selected Interest Rates (www.federalreserve.gov/releases/h15/current/default.htm).

Carney, Mark. 2012. "Guidance." Speech to CFA Society Toronto, Toronto, Ontario (December 11) (www.bankofcanada.ca/wp-content/uploads/2012/12/remarks-111212.pdf).

Chen, Han, Vasco Cúrdia, and Andrea Ferrero. 2012. "The Macroeconomic Effects of Large-Scale Asset Purchase Programmes." *The Economic Journal* 122, no. 564: F289–F315.

Christensen, Jens, and Glenn Rudebusch. 2012. "The Response of Interest Rates to US and UK Quantitative Easing." *Economic Journal* 122: F385–F414.

Chung, Hess, and others. 2012. "Have We Underestimated the Probability of Hitting the Zero Lower Bound?" *Journal of Money, Credit and Banking* 44: 47–82.

Coenen, Günter, Athanasios Orphanides, and Volker Wieland. 2004. "Price Stability and Monetary Policy Effectiveness When Nominal Interest Rates Are Bounded at Zero." *Advances in Macroeconomics* 4, no. 1: 1–23.

Coenen, Günter, and Volker Wieland. 2004. "Exchange-Rate Policy and the Zero Lower Bound on Nominal Interest Rates." *American Economic Review Paper and Proceedings* 94, no. 2: 80–84.

D'Amico, Stefania, and others. 2012. "The Federal Reserve's Large-Scale Asset Purchase Programmes: Rationale and Effects." *Economic Journal* 122: F415–46.

D'Amico, Stefania, and Thomas King. 2013. "Flow and Stock Effects of Large-Scale Treasury Purchases: Evidence on the Importance of Local Supply." *Journal of Financial Economics* 108, no. 2: 425–48.

Eggertsson, Gauti B., and Michael Woodford. 2003. "The Zero Bound on Interest Rates and Optimal Monetary Policy." *Brookings Papers on Economic Activity* (Spring), pp. 139–211.

Federal Reserve Bank of New York. 2013. Primary Dealer Surveys (www.new yorkfed.org/markets/primarydealer_survey_questions.html).

Femia, Katherine, Steven Friedman, and Brian Sack. 2013. "The Effects of Policy Guidance on Perceptions of the Fed's Reaction Function." Federal Reserve Bank of New York Staff Report 652 (November).

Gagnon, Joseph, and others. 2011. "The Financial Market Effects of the Federal Reserve's Large-Scale Asset Purchases." *International Journal of Central Banking* 7: 3–43.

Greenwood, Robin, and Dimitri Vayanos. 2008. "Bond Supply and Excess Bond Returns." Working Paper 13806. Cambridge, Mass.: National Bureau of Economic Research,.

Gürkaynak, Refet, Brian Sack, and Eric Swanson. 2005. "Do Actions Speak Louder than Words? The Response of Asset Prices to Monetary Policy Actions and Statements." *International Journal of Central Banking* 1: 55–93.

Hamilton, James, and Jing Cynthia Wu. 2011. "The Effectiveness of Alternative Monetary Policy Tools in a Zero Lower Bound Environment." *Journal of Money, Credit, and Banking* 44: 3–46.

Hancock, Diana, and Wayne Passmore. 2011. "Did the Federal Reserve's MBS Purchase Program Lower Mortgage Rates?" *Journal of Monetary Economics* 58, no. 5:. 498–514.

Jordà, Òscar, Moritz Schularick, and Alan M. Taylor. 2011. "Financial Crises, Credit Booms, and External Imbalances: 140 Years of Lessons." *IMF Economic Review*, vol. 59, pp. 340–78.

Joyce, Michael, and others. 2011. "The Financial Market Impact of Quantitative Easing." *International Journal of Central Banking* 7, no. 3: 113–61.

Krishnamurthy, Arvind, and Annette Vissing-Jorgensen. 2011. "The Effects of Quantitative Easing on Interest Rates." *Brookings Papers on Economic Activity* (Fall), pp. 215–65.

———. 2012. "The Aggregate Demand for Treasury Debt." *Journal of Political Economy* 120, no. 2: pp. 233–67.

Laubach, Thomas, and John C. Williams. 2003. "Measuring the Natural Rate of Interest." (With Thomas Laubach.) *Review of Economics and Statistics* 85, no. 4 (November): 1063–70.

Li, Canlin, and Min Wei. 2013. "Term Structure Modeling with Supply Factors and the Federal Reserve's Large-Scale Asset Purchase Programs." *International Journal of Central Banking* 9, no. 1: pp. 3–39.

McCallum, Bennett T. 2000. "Theoretical Analysis Regarding a Zero Lower Bound on Nominal Interest Rates." *Journal of Money, Credit and Banking* 32 (November): 870–904.

McGough, Bruce, Glenn D. Rudebusch, and John C. Williams. 2005. "Using a Long-Term Interest Rate as the Monetary Policy Instrument." *Journal of Monetary Economics* 52 (July): 855–79.

Modigliani, Franco, and Richard Sutch. 1966. "Innovations in Interest Rate Policy." *American Economic Review* 56: 178–97.

———. 1967. "Debt Management and the Term Structure of Interest Rates: An Empirical Analysis of Recent Experience." *Journal of Political Economy* 75: 569–89.

Neely, Christopher J. 2013. "Unconventional Monetary Policy Had Large International Effects." Working Paper 2010-018D. Federal Reserve Bank of St. Louis, August.

Organization for Economic Cooperation and Development (OECD). (2013). OECD. StatExtracts. (http://stats.oecd.org/Index.aspx?DatasetCode=MEI_FIN).

Reifschneider, David, and John M. Roberts. 2006. "Expectations Formation and the Effectiveness of Strategies for Limiting the Consequences of the Zero Bound." *Journal of the Japanese and International Economies* 20 (September): 314–37.

Reifschneider, David, and John C. Williams. 2000. "Three Lessons for Monetary Policy in a Low Inflation Era." *Journal of Money, Credit and Banking* 32 (November): 936–66.

———. 2002. "FOMC Briefing." Board of Governors of the Federal Reserve System, Washington, D.C. (January).

Reinhart, Carmen M., and Kenneth S. Rogoff. 2009. "The Aftermath of Financial Crises." Working Paper 14656. Cambridge, Mass.: National Bureau of Economic Research.

Rudebusch, Glenn D., and John C. Williams. 2008. "Revealing the Secrets of the Temple: The Value of Publishing Central Bank Interest Rate Projections." In *Asset Prices and Monetary Policy*, edited by John Y. Campbell, pp. 247–84. University of Chicago Press.

Schmitt-Grohé, Stephanie, and Martín Uribe. 2007. "Optimal Inflation Stabilization in a Medium-Scale Macroeconomic Model." In *Monetary Policy under Inflation Targeting*, edited by Klaus Schmidt-Hebbel and Rick Mishkin, pp. 125–86. Santiago: Central Bank of Chile.

Svensson, Lars E. O. 2001. "The Zero Bound in an Open Economy: A Foolproof Way of Escaping from a Liquidity Trap." *Monetary and Economic Studies* 19 (February): 277–312.

Swanson, Eric T. 2011. "Let's Twist Again: A High-Frequency Event-Study Analysis of Operation Twist and Its Implications for QE2." *Brookings Papers on Economic Activity* (Spring), pp. 151–88.

Swanson, Eric T., and John C. Williams. 2012. "Measuring the Effect of the Zero Lower Bound on Medium- and Longer-Term Interest Rates." Working Paper 2012-02. Federal Reserve Bank of San Francisco (February).

———. 2013. "Measuring the Effect of the Zero Lower Bound on Yields and Exchange Rates in the U.K. and Germany." Working Paper 2013-21. Federal Reserve Bank of San Francisco (August).

Taylor, John B. 1993. "Discretion versus Policy Rules in Practice." *Carnegie-Rochester Conference Series on Public Policy*, vol. 39, pp. 195–214.

Vayanos, Dimitri, and Jean-Luc Vila. 2009. "A Preferred-Habitat Model of the Term Structure of Interest Rates." Working Paper 15487. Cambridge, Mass.: National Bureau of Economic Research.

Williams, John C. 2006. "Monetary Policy in a Low Inflation Economy with Learning." In *Monetary Policy in an Environment of Low Inflation; Proceedings of the Bank of Korea International Conference 2006*, pp. 199–228. Seoul: The Bank of Korea.

———. 2009. "Heeding Daedalus: Optimal Inflation and the Zero Lower Bound." *Brookings Papers on Economic Activity* (Fall 2009), pp. 1–37.

———. 2013a. "A Defense of Moderation in Monetary Policy." *Journal of Macroeconomics* 38 (December): 137–50.

———. 2013b. "Lessons from the Financial Crisis for Unconventional Monetary Policy." Presentation at NBER Conference, "Lessons from the Financial Crisis for Monetary Policy." National Bureau of Economic Research, Cambridge, Mass., October 18.

Woodford, Michael. 2013. "Forward Guidance by Inflation-Targeting Central Banks." *Sveriges Riksbank Economic Review* 3: 81–120.

World Bank. 2013. World Economic Indicators (http://data.worldbank.org/indicator/NY.GDP.PCAP.K).

DISCUSSION

Martin Feldstein of Harvard University responded to John Williams's presentation, and then David Wessel moderated a discussion and took questions from the audience that included comments by Paul Tucker, former deputy governor of the Bank of England, as well as from two journalists.

FELDSTEIN: John Williams's very insightful paper deals with the proper conduct of monetary policy under the protracted adverse conditions of the kind that we have experienced since 2006. Although we might hope that such conditions won't happen again, John presents persuasive historic evidence that such declines in aggregate demand are indeed likely to recur, so it's important that we learn from recent experience and consider alternative policies.

The 2007 downturn was not only deeper and longer than the usual recession, but also differed in its origin and structure. It was not caused by temporarily high real interest rates and therefore couldn't be reversed by the Fed's usual rate reduction. Even at a near zero federal funds rate, the recession persisted.

The downturn was caused by a mispricing of the risks of a wide range of assets. Individuals bought overpriced homes, and banks gave high-value mortgages to individuals who were unable to repay them. House prices began to collapse in the summer of 2006, causing a massive fall in household wealth and residential construction.

Banks and other investors bought overpriced tranches of securitized subprime mortgages that then collapsed in value, signaling the general overpricing of risky securities. In many cases, banks and other financial institutions couldn't even determine the value of their portfolio assets because of the lack of willing buyers and sellers. Banks therefore couldn't know the value of their own capital and couldn't judge the solvency of potential counterparties. The financial markets became dysfunctional, and credit dried up.

The Federal Reserve and the Treasury together acted very boldly to revive financial markets with a combination of assets purchases and guarantees that went far beyond monetary policy. Although these actions succeeded in reversing the financial collapse, they didn't reverse the economic downturn.

The Federal Reserve also cut the Fed funds rate to near zero in late 2008, too late to satisfy John's suggestion "to act aggressively in cutting rates when a sharp decline in output threatens." That would have implied cutting rates in 2006 when house prices began to collapse, but the Fed funds rate was still nearly 5 percent in the fall of 2007.

In analyzing the challenges in 2007 and 2008, it's important to go beyond simulations using the fat tails implied by historic data. Traditional macroeconometric models cannot begin to capture the problems in 2007 because they lack a well-specified financial sector—let alone the securitization of mortgages into tranches— and don't recognize the widespread presence of off-balance sheets' special investment vehicles. Moreover, all financial crises may not share the same features.

Although this meeting is about monetary policy, I think it's wrong to ignore the role of fiscal policy at the zero lower bound. Conventional wisdom before 2007 was that cyclical fluctuations should be managed by monetary policy alone because countercyclical fiscal policy is generally too slow to react within the typical recession downturn.

But in 2007 several of us concluded that current conditions implied that a fiscal stimulus was needed. Unfortunately, the Bush tax cut of 2008 was totally ineffective because it was a small one-time rebate that households almost entirely saved. The Obama stimulus plan of 2009 probably dampened the downturn, but was too small and not concentrated enough on increasing government spending.

With an inadequate fiscal policy, the Fed was the only hope for stimulating the economy. With the Fed funds rate at the zero lower bound, the Fed shifted to unconventional monetary policy, a future or forward guidance of the short rate, and large-scale asset purchases (LSAPs) of government bonds and mortgage-backed securities.

John provides a very useful review of the evaluation of the future guidance. He concludes from it, "explicit forward guidance can effectively anchor interest rate expectations out two years." But I ask myself, why is a two-year anchoring economically significant? The usefulness of forward guidance would be persuasive if it reduced the longer-term rates that are relevant for mortgages and equity prices.

John reminds us that the standard textbook theory implies that LSAPs cannot affect asset prices and interest rates. We now know that that theory is wrong. The Fed's massive purchases of Treasury bonds and mortgage-backed securities drove the yield on ten-year Treasuries to just 1.7 percent in May of 2013. The announced plan to end the purchase program was enough to drive that rate back to 3 percent.

John quotes research showing that the $600 billion bond purchase in QE2 lowered the unemployment rate by one-quarter of 1 percent, but he's candid in concluding that there remains "a great deal of uncertainty about the magnitude of these effects, and their impact on the overall economy."

Missing in all of this analysis is a balancing of the potential output gains of LSAPs against the risks generated by sustaining abnormally lower long-term interest rates. Those risks include: (1) potential price bubbles in equities, land, and other assets; (2) portfolio risks as investors reach for yield with junk bonds, emerging market debt, uncovered options, and the like; (3) creditor risks as lenders make loans to less qualified borrowers, covenant light loans and bonds, long-term mortgages at insufficient interest rates, and so on; and (4) long-term inflation risk as commercial banks acquire a large portfolio of low-yielding assets at the Federal Reserve that could be converted to commercial loans.

In his conclusion, John asks whether LSAPs should be a standard tool when short rates are at the zero lower bound. I think it is too soon to tell. We will know more when we see the outcomes of the risks that the LSAPs created. If the economy now expands at a healthy pace, at which I think we've got a good shot, we won't know what those risk outcomes would have been in a weaker economy.

What is clear to me is that a balanced fiscal policy should be part of the response when the economy is stuck with excess capacity at the zero lower bound.

Finally, John asks whether it would be better to target nominal GDP, the price level, or an inflation rate higher than 2 percent. I think any of those would be a mistake.

Although inflation is not a problem now, the time will come when the Fed will want to limit or reverse inflationary pressures. Experience and theory both teach that it is easier to do that if the public understands that the Federal Reserve is committed to a consistent policy of low inflation. Flirting now with other more ambiguous goals can only weaken future public support when the Fed needs it most.

WESSEL: John, when you described history, you didn't mention fiscal policy. But we know that fiscal policy was a big player, and to quote Ben

Bernanke, was "counterproductive."[11] So when we get to an episode like this, what is the right thing for the monetary policy authority to do? Do you compensate for lousy fiscal policy and do more? Or do you say to the Congress and the president: look, we're doing what we have done and publicly indict fiscal policymakers for not doing the right thing?

WILLIAMS: First of all, I don't think fiscal policy was lousy. We actually had pretty sizable fiscal stimulus. More would have been better. The fact that it has turned the other way obviously is more of a negative.

From the point of view of monetary policy, you have to take fiscal policy realities—and the political realities that come with that—as a given, and then we have to calibrate monetary policy as best we can to achieve our mandated goals from Congress: maximum employment and stable prices.

That said, I agree completely that the leadership of the Federal Reserve can and should speak clearly and forcefully about the beneficial effects of countercyclical fiscal policy, especially at the zero lower bound. That's a message that most economists would agree on and is obviously logical and makes a lot of sense. But there is the reality that Washington does what it does, and we have to try our best given the hand we're dealt.

WESSEL: What about the risk that what you're doing now is sowing the seeds of the next bout of financial instability?

WILLIAMS: We take this very seriously. Obviously, we've all learned the lessons of the past decade or so. We follow very carefully what's happening in financial markets, both in the banking part of the financial system and in the capital markets. You have to think about the shadow banking system and the rest of the system. We have increased our monitoring and our analysis.

The first line of defense regarding issues of growing financial risks is around micro- and macroprudential policies. We should be developing both, having the right policies, and implementing them. We made incredibly important strides in terms of financial stability, in terms of the stress tests, and in terms of our implementation of Dodd-Frank.

---

11. Ben S. Bernanke, speaking at the Annual Meeting of the American Economic Association, Philadelphia, January 2, 2014 (www.federalreserve.gov/newsevents/speech/bernanke 20140103a.htm).

We are balancing the costs and benefits around our quantitative easing policies. And the macroeconomic benefits far outweigh some of these issues right now.

Broadly defined, our financial system is still in a risk-averse mode, not a risk-loving mode. You can find specific examples of farmland prices or leveraged-loan prices, but these concerns today are not as prevalent as some people think.

TUCKER: I agree with Marty's conclusion of "don't give up on inflation targeting." That battle is hard won, and it constantly needs to be reaffirmed. But central banks elsewhere in the world are puzzled by the Fed's approach to quantitative easing. You're not deciding on a stock of money that you want to put out there, and then review it after a while to determine whether you've done enough, just as you would set an interest rate and leave it, and then decide after a while whether you've done enough. Instead you've had this policy of "we'll trickle it out there" on a flow basis.

WILLIAMS: We've been trying different approaches on that—QE1 and QE2. QE2 was a concrete example of a $600 billion purchase over a certain specific period of time. It provides a lot of certainty in markets, and markets like certainty. It provides a lot of bang for the buck in the sense that when you make the announcement, the market reaction occurs immediately. There are positives to that and there's clarity around it.

That is not how monetary policy should be conducted. Monetary policy should be conducted by adjusting your instruments as the economic conditions and the economic outlook evolve.

One of the lessons we learned from those earlier episodes is that we were surprised that the economy did not do as well as we thought. We needed to introduce a new program: QE2, then Operation Twist, then QE3.

This more open-ended policy, in which markets come to their own conclusions and analysis about how big the policy eventually will be, had the advantage that the policy can be automatically adjusted both in size, compensation, and duration as economic conditions change. That's why we laid out this substantial improvement threshold for the outlook for the labor market.[12]

---

12 See www.federalreserve.gov/newsevents/press/monetary/20130731a.htm).

The economy didn't do as well as we thought, and we've been doing these purchases longer than people originally thought. Because of a change in economic conditions and the outlook, we're doing far more than the initial $600 billion. And that's exactly what we should be doing, given what has happened with the economy. As with the taper, we're adjusting that on the basis of the improvement in economic conditions.

The natural thing to do is to adjust your policy instruments as the economic outlook changes. That said, I do recognize that it creates quite a bit of uncertainty. When will the Fed stop its purchases? When will it taper? We had the famous taper tantrum last year. And it was something we learned from.

We learned that when you have a $600 billion policy, you don't have the flexibility to adjust it as economic conditions change. And that's a weakness. We've also learned that there are a lot of communication challenges and confusion when you have an open-ended policy with relatively vague conditions for bringing it to an end. This is something that we need to think more about.

GREG IP (*The Economist*): The real output effects of quantitative easing that you identified were based on models that link the decline in long-term interest rates to the output effects. As you and Marty have both said, we have vastly misunderstood this linkage and the role that the financial system plays in terms of changing interest rates and what that actually does to the economy.

You could make the case that in the last four or five years, frictions in the financial markets have blocked the normal transmission of monetary policy. So doesn't that weaken the empirical link that you've drawn between the effect of quantitative easing and the impact on the real economy?

WILLIAMS: Absolutely. If you think of the U.S. economy as an eight-cylinder auto engine, several of the cylinders were clogged shortly after the financial crisis. I think they're getting less clogged now.

That said, there's no question that both lowering interest rate expectations of the next couple of years through forward guidance, and through quantitative easing over the five- and ten-year horizon, has lowered mortgage rates, auto rates, and corporate borrowing rates. In what parts of the economy are we seeing the biggest improvement? Autos, durable goods, and the housing market.

The monetary transmission mechanism has been partly clogged over the last few years. At that same time, the very aggressive policies have had an effect and have gotten traction, and I think they are a really important part of the economy improving.

JON HILSENRATH (*Wall Street Journal*): The Fed employed a low-for-longer approach to interest rates after the tech bubble burst. Several years later, we had a housing bubble. What is the risk that a low-for-longer policy could contribute to bubbles? Does it disturb you that the Michael Woodford models, upon which low-for-longer is based, don't take much account of the creation of bubbles?[13] And how should this factor into the Fed's thinking now as it employs a low-for-longer policy again?

WILLIAMS: The models that we use do not take seriously that there's a complex financial system out there that can have endogenous changes in leverage and risk taking. Our models tend to assume highly rational agents who have a full understanding of things, so bubbles never occur.

We have to broaden our minds to more of an approach that allows for the possibility that asset markets can get away from fundamentals for specific periods of time and that financial markets can get disrupted.

My answer to your question is that I don't think that the lower interest rates were an important contributor to the housing bubble. I think fundamentally flawed aspects of our regulatory environment were the key part of that story about the housing bubble. The Dodd-Frank legislation, Basel III, and a lot of the other things we're doing are addressing those concerns in a very important way.

We have to have open minds about understanding how low interest rates for a long period of time do affect risk taking, leverage, and asset prices, as Marty said.

ABBY JOSEPH COHEN (Goldman Sachs, trustee of the Brookings Institution): Marty Feldstein made a very interesting comment that all the Fed needed to do was mention taper and the financial markets adjusted. The biggest adjustment wasn't in the United States; it was in emerging markets, especially emerging-market debt. This raises the question of what is it that we don't know about the linkage, not just between our financial markets and monetary policy, but also markets around the

13. See Michael Woodford, "Methods of Policy Accommodation at the Interest-Rate Lower Bound," September 16, 2012 (www.kansascityfed.org/publicat/sympos/2012/mw.pdf?sm=jh083112-4).

world? Specifically, what do we think now about the interplay of central bank policy from different nations? And also, the regulatory difference, particularly with regard to the supervision of financial institutions?

WILLIAMS: We saw hot money flows going to emerging-market countries during the last few years, and we saw big swings in those flows when the discussion of tapering took place. From my perspective, the most important thing is that we're communicating very effectively across the globe with our central bank colleagues, and that communication includes understanding what our policies are and what our intentions are.

As we've seen the last few years, the countries that have been affected in a major important way by these flows have adapted their policies and their approaches to better insulate them from some of those effects. At the end of the day, we live in a modern, global financial system. This is just part of the world that we live in. Monetary policy in the United States is obviously having effects outside the United States, and we need to study those. We need to understand those, and we need to coordinate or communicate effectively with our colleagues around the world.

FELDSTEIN: The only thing I would add is that the Fed doesn't take those effects on other countries into account.

TUCKER: They should—to the extent that there is a risk that it will flow back into the United States. What you're describing is the cross-border, cross-currency carry/trade. It's been ignored in the economics profession and in central banking for far too long. And it doesn't just flow one way; it can bounce back. The worst of the euro area crisis demonstrated that the linkages of the world don't just run from here to there—they can flow back as well.

4

REGULATORY REFORM
What's Done? What Isn't?

PAUL TUCKER

The crisis that broke in 2007 and brought the international financial system to its knees in late 2008, threatening a repeat of the Great Depression, left the credibility of financial regulation and supervision in tatters. Until this is repaired, confidence in the financial system itself will remain fragile.

Of course there were plenty of other factors behind the crisis: a badly unbalanced global economy, with much of the West owing too much to the high-saving economies of the East; a rampant search for yield associated with declining global real interest rates and persistently easy monetary conditions; myopia about risk; soporific reliance on highly liquid markets; herding, on the way up as well as, later, to the exit; moral hazard from a perceived and, as it turned out, available taxpayer safety net; and a legion of agency problems in banks and investment managers.

Those agency problems were serious, with no one stopping dealers and banks from expanding their balance sheets to maintain, or increase,

My thanks to Svein Andresen, Dick Berner, Steve Cecchetti, Darrell Duffie, Randy Guynne, Sam Hanson, Don Kohn, Eric Rosengren, Vicky Saporta, David Scharfstein, Hal Scott, Andrei Shleifer, David Wessel, and participants in a Harvard Business School seminar for comments and discussions. Thank you to Asfandyar Nadeem for the graphics. Views and mistakes are my own.

leverage as rising asset prices inflated the value of their equity.[1] Others—in all types of banking, and throughout the West—gradually adopted copycat strategies under pressure from their boards and stockholders. Risk was underpriced. The resulting credit boom left many borrowers overindebted and assets overvalued.

But the crisis would not have been as deep, nor its economic effects so long lasting, if the core of the financial system had not been fatally weak. Economies can survive overvalued property markets and overindebted borrowers if their financial systems are able to weather the losses and thus maintain the supply of credit. They couldn't.

Key money markets dried up. So few banks held reliably liquid assets, so many were excessively reliant on skittish short-term funding, so many had promised liquidity insurance to off-balance sheet vehicles that found their market funding cut off, that central banks were acting as lenders of last resort (LOLR) from mid-2007—before anything much had happened in the real world.

Even though the liquidity fragility inherent in the mismatch between short-term liabilities and longer-term assets was the very point of regulating banking in the first place, it should have been remarkable that the whole system could be pushed over the edge by small losses originating in the U.S. subprime mortgage market. Opacity created uncertainty about which securities were tarnished and who held damaged portfolios. A complex network of credit exposures among banks and other financial institutions prompted concerns that, at least indirectly, pretty well everybody was exposed. But surely the fatal fault line was the woeful undercapitalization of the banks (and their "shadow-banking" cousins), tipping some over the edge as the storm broke and, crucially for the economy, leaving the banking system incapable of reintermediating the provision of credit as capital markets closed. Although undoubtedly exacerbated by the liquidity crisis that began in 2007, too many firms were unsound to begin with.

1. See Adrian and Shin (2010). They study a process working through the marking-to-market of assets, but other mechanisms involved gearing up with term debt on the back of unusually profitable commercial banking operations, increasing risk exposures as value-at-risk measures fell due to declining volatility, and heavy use of securitization as an apparently cheap funding source (as in the case of Northern Rock in the United Kingdom). Each instance combines misperceptions of the durability of unusual market conditions, myopia about tail risk, and weak incentives to wake up.

While borrowers and lenders were responsible for their own imprudence, responsibility for the stability of the system as a whole lay squarely with the authorities. This was a failure of prudential supervision and regulation on a grand scale—on both sides of the Atlantic. The authorities had been blind to the buildup of banking-type risks—leverage and maturity transformation—outside of de jure banks. And to pile on the agony, they failed to see that the banking system needed heightened resilience given global macroeconomic imbalances, unusually low risk-free real interest rates and elevated asset values, compressed risk premiums in credit markets, and accumulating household debt. The macrofinancial feedbacks were more vicious in the bust for having been ignored in the boom.

Cross-border contagion was rife. Notwithstanding well-documented lessons from the Asian crisis of the 1990s, the pattern of gross capital flows and the consequent structure of external liabilities and claims (the national balance sheet) were barely monitored, let alone managed.[2] A good example is euro area banks investing in risky U.S. securities, funded by flighty U.S. money market funds.

Perhaps worst of all, when the bust came, no country had the technology to resolve large and complex financial institutions.[3] Although part of the problem was that the writ of the Federal Deposit Insurance Corporation (FDIC) did not then run to broker dealers or holding companies—a problem partly cured by the Dodd-Frank Act—in fact the traditional "purchase and assumption" technique for separating firms into their critical and other parts would not remotely have coped with the failure of the more complex commercial banks.[4] Elsewhere, it was

2. This is extraordinary given the 2000 Report of the Financial Stability Forum Working Group on Capital Flows, which was presented to G-7 and G-20 Ministers (Financial Stability Forum 2000). It urged controlling vulnerabilities in national balance sheets, highlighting lessons from the Asian crisis about gross indebtedness in different sectors, not net current account imbalances. This was not absorbed by macroeconomic policymakers and was too "macro" for regulators.

3. This is despite a joint G-10/Financial Stability Forum (2001) report on the problems of winding down large and complex financial institutions (or LCFIs, as systemically important financial institutions [SIFIs] were then called). The report was not published at the time but was presented to ministers.

4. The standard technique for resolving a standard bank involves splitting off the insured-deposit book and transferring it to a healthy competitor. Broadly, other services are regarded as noncritical. That is not true for many big firms offering complex services.

much worse: the United Kingdom had no resolution regime at all. When this was realized, the withdrawal of funding snowballed. The consequent taxpayer bailouts of 2008–09 raised moral hazard to new heights.

A CORE INTERNATIONAL REFORM PROGRAM

Although at times preoccupied with local reform debates, the capitals of the world's major economies confronted common issues in redrawing the rules of the road for finance. Combined with a shared desire to preserve open, global financial markets, this has meant the main reform action has been international—perhaps more so than is recognized in the United States or in London. Overall, the test is whether the reforms can increase the resilience of the system as a whole, reduce contagion when trouble hits, and mitigate the pro-cyclicality of financial conditions.

Broadly, the *banking package* is coherent and well-conceived, seeking to address excess leverage, excess opacity, excess interconnectedness, excess maturity mismatches, as well as the biggest issue of all: too big to fail (TBTF; see figure 4-1). The aim is to apply its key elements not only to de jure banks, but also to any important institutions that are leveraged and exposed to liquidity runs. Higher solvency requirements and a credible regime for resolving distressed firms will, taken together, reduce the risk of panicky liquidity runs and, in the event that a run does occur, make it easier to restore order without a bailout.

This evaluation therefore begins with the four core planks of the international reform effort, which is broadly consistent with the Dodd-Frank legislation in the United States:[5]

—Strengthening the balance sheets of banks and revitalizing prudential supervision.

—Ensuring that distress at any financial institution can be resolved in an orderly way without taxpayer *solvency* support, that is, *no bailouts*.

—Guarding against endemic regulatory arbitrage undermining those efforts, so that shadow banking is not left free to blow up the financial system at some point in the future.

---

5. See, for example, the Financial Stability Board chair's letter to G-20 leaders (FSB 2013d), September 2013.

FIGURE 4-1. Banking Reforms

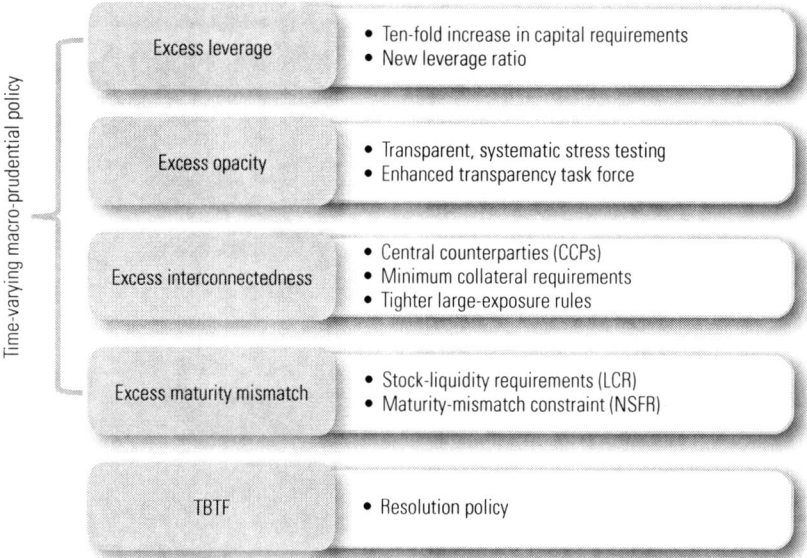

Note: LCR = liquidity coverage ratio; NSFR = net stable funding ratio; TBTF = too big to fail.

—Simplifying the network of counterparty credit exposures among banks and dealers, through mandated use of central counterparties (CCPs) for standard derivatives.

The discussion of those reforms in the next section leaves hanging in the air some big questions about whether rewriting the social contract for banking is sufficient to preserve systemic stability; and, relatedly, whether it is enough to focus on institutions rather than also on markets or activities. This matters because policy on markets is somewhat less coherent, vigorous, and joined-up, although arguably less immediately pressing. Those issues are then examined alongside a possible framework for markets policy that distinguishes between capital markets and money markets and therefore identifies four overlapping but distinct policy spheres (see figure 4-2). The rebuilding of regulatory institutions is discussed next, with the emphasis on nimble and flexible regulation (given rules arbitrage, innovation, and "cyclical" variations in credit conditions), broader objectives for securities regulators, the challenges

FIGURE 4-2. Not Just about Banking
(A Mistake to Focus Everything on SIFIs)

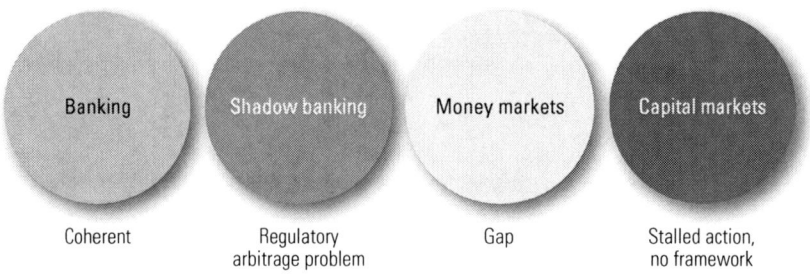

Banking	Shadow banking	Money markets	Capital markets
Coherent	Regulatory arbitrage problem	Gap	Stalled action, no framework

facing "macroprudential" institutions, and reforms that can help to meet concerns about the legitimacy of central bank support operations.

THE SAFETY AND SOUNDNESS OF BANKS: FROM MICRO- TO MACROPRUDENTIAL SUPERVISION ANDREGULATION

Not banning maturity transformation and credit extension in banks is surely right. By combining the provision of demand deposits with committed lines of credit, banking delivers efficiency gains in the management of liquidity risk for households and firms;[6] otherwise, everybody would have to stockpile liquidity themselves all the time. But making banks self-insure by holding *some* reliably liquid assets that can be drawn down when needed has long been overdue. Also sensible is Basel's planned net stable funding requirement, which will constrain maturity mismatch by limiting the proportion of banks' assets that can be funded short term. Although calibration is difficult given the state of knowledge, these measures take some pressure off capital policy.

Even so, the best safeguard against liquidity panics is for funders and counterparties to see that banks hold adequate capital against their risks; resilient solvency is the best liquidity policy. The new Basel Accord is rightly focused on *equity* capital, with a requirement of around 10 percent for the biggest international banking groups—the so-called

6. See Kayshap, Rajan, and Stein (2002).

systemically important financial institutions (SIFIs). Some query whether that is enough. But it is an order of magnitude higher than the previous minimum of around 1 percent (as measured today),[7] so would have dampened somewhat the excesses of the mid-2000s boom, as well as provided considerably greater cover against losses. Moreover, reforms are, I trust, on course to raise the equity cover for potentially illiquid trading positions, which is tremendously important in a world where sharp increases in liquidity premiums on marked-to-market assets can drive a bank or dealer over an accountant's definition of solvency. Nevertheless, this minimum capital ratio would be insufficient on its own, so policymakers have a package that ranges from technical repairs, through a backstop and state-contingent macro-prudential variations in parameters, to an overhaul of resolution regimes.

If risk weights were driven wholly by banks' own models, the capital in the system could again end up being too low, reflecting banks' private interests rather than the wider needs of the economy. Supervisors plan to expose and reduce unwarranted variations in firms' risk models. More fundamentally, work is under way to simplify the framework. The solution should be common floors on risk weights—a regime somewhere between Basel II and the broad-brush constraints of the mid-1980s' Basel I.

Rather than rely on improving the integrity of risk-asset ratios, the 2009 London Summit decided to apply a cap to leverage, that is, total assets/equity. It, too, would be insufficient on its own, inducing firms to move into high-risk businesses that looked low risk to regulators and bondholders.[8] It will be a backstop—one that will bite on those firms whose business is heavily concentrated in activities carrying very low risk weights.

---

7. Equivalently, in "old money," the increase is much more than 10 percent. A key improvement in the accord is the deduction from equity of more items, including goodwill and investments in insurance subsidiaries. This gets much closer to "free capital" that can absorb losses in a going concern and affects measures of leverage, too. Other components of "Tier 1" and "Total" capital are more relevant to resolution, since they affect the creditor hierarchy for the absorption of losses in insolvency. The accord needs further revision to recognize this vital distinction between *going-concern* and *gone-concern loss-absorbing capacity*. See further discussion in this section.

8. An example is lending to Latin American and East European sovereigns in the late 1970s to early 1980s, when a leverage limit was the main constraint on bank balance sheets. See Duffie (2013).

But whether the minimum risk-asset ratio was 10 percent, 15 percent, or 20 percent, or the leverage cap 33x or 25x, a static regulatory capital requirement of this kind will not prove sufficient for every state of the world. This is driving moves to a richer *macroprudential* regime capable of adjusting requirements where warranted by changing economic and financial conditions.

Time-Varying Macroprudential Policy:
Credit Cycles and Regulatory Flexibility

"Cyclical" variation of headline or sector-exposure capital (and other) requirements is a completely new dimension of the regulatory settlement. It is too often caricatured as almost absurdly ambitious: manage the credit cycle; employ robust, scientific criteria for identifying bubbles; find the optimal combination of macroprudential and monetary instrument settings.

While those should be long-term goals, there is a more modest way of approaching policy in the meantime—by framing the primary goal as *sustaining the resilience of the financial system* in the face of material changes in financial and economic conditions. If the environment became a lot more risky than contemplated when the parameters of the base regulatory framework were determined, or if a boom were inflating the accounting equity of intermediaries,[9] the desired degree of resilience could be preserved by temporarily increasing minimum capital requirements (or, as discussed in a later section here, minimum collateral requirements). In other words, build up buffers in the good times. This might be as important for clusters of medium-sized firms with correlated exposures as it is for SIFIs. It might or might not dampen a boom, but the bust would be milder than otherwise because the financial system would be more able to bear the losses. A debt overhang would still impede the subsequent macroeconomic recovery, but the downturn would be less severe if banking does not collapse.

There is exaggerated pessimism about spotting vulnerabilities from credit-fueled booms. Absolutely nothing is foolproof, but policymakers need to be open to placing weight on anecdotal evidence alongside rigorous analysis. Chuck Prince was not the first to point to the problem of

9. See Adrian and Shin (2010).

leaving the dance floor while the music was still playing. Before the bust in 2007, Wall Street risk managers saw individual firms as facing a difficult choice between financial risk (a runaway credit boom) and business risk (withdrawing from a market before an uncertain bust, only to see their franchise destroyed as business moved to their competitors).[10] This was a powerful signal of a collective action problem. Timely macroprudential interventions (not empty talk) can potentially act as a coordinating device for intermediaries to exit the dance floor together, helping to dampen the pro-cyclical dynamic of a system left to its own devices.

The introduction of macroprudential policy (macropru) fills a gap, permitting a better overall policy mix. In relation to monetary policy, macropru is the first mover. It needs to take account of monetary influences on risk-taking behavior, but leave monetary policy itself freer to concentrate on managing the path of nominal demand in pursuit of an inflation target. And in relation to micro-regulatory policy, the basic requirements need not be calibrated for the very worst states of the world given that they can be temporarily increased where warranted. That weighed in Basel III, reducing inadvertent risks to long-run economic growth.[11]

Of course, there will be challenges. At times regulators will need the will, as recently, to overcome banks' reluctance to raise new equity, in order to contain economically destructive deleveraging. More profoundly, macroprudential policy can hardly work unless regulators can judge how robust or vulnerable the system is in the face of gathering threats. Systematic stress testing can transform those assessments, potentially bringing about a revolution in prudential supervision.

Systematic, Transparent Stress Testing: A Revolution in Supervision

The Federal Reserve has led the world in introducing credible tests of banks' capital adequacy. As well as being forward looking and focused

---

10. Market intelligence to that effect was fed into official systemic-risk assessments; for example, see Bank of England (2006), pp. 8 and 30. Another example is the telecom company debt boom in the early 2000s. The euphoria could be picked up while queuing for morning coffee on Wall Street or in the city, but it almost felled some major global banks in late 2002 in a widely neglected near-crisis.

11. For research reaching a similar conclusion, see Aghion and Kharroubi (2013).

on tail risk, they are annual, concurrent, systematic, and, by any previous standard of supervision, highly transparent. They aid an assessment of resilience by taking into account correlated exposures across firms. Other jurisdictions are following. Alongside greater disclosures by banks themselves, these reforms can reduce the opacity of banking, aiding more discriminating market discipline.[12] And if eventually more account can be taken of feedback mechanisms, the tests can be more *macroprudential*.[13]

Within central banks, modern stress testing entails bank supervisors and macroeconomists working together. If sustained, this will be a remarkable achievement under Chairman Ben Bernanke's watch, helping to break down cultural silos and thus to make a success of combining in one institution the two dimensions of maintaining a stable monetary system: price stability and banking stability.

The transparency is necessary given the damaged reputation of supervisors.[14] But its greatest long-term benefit may be to transform public accountability for prudential supervision. Year by year, everyone will see the severity of the chosen stress scenarios as well as the results, and legislators will be able to examine regulators on both. This takes a step toward the kind of accountability familiar in monetary policy. Supervision need no longer be a mystery, of interest and accessible to the public and their representatives only when something goes badly wrong.

But none of these benefits will be secured unless the authorities have technically feasible and credible choices, other than taxpayer bailout, when a transparent asset-quality review or stress test reveals a banking group to be abjectly weak. The European Union stress tests a few years ago demonstrated that.

Resolution: Solving Too Big to Fail and Future Constraints on Bank Balance Sheet Structure

This matters hugely because improvements in bank regulation and supervision will not consign distress to the dustbin. Should it be thought that this problem could be overcome by applying a

---

12. Notably, the measures recommended by the private sector Enhanced Disclosure Task Force.

13. See, for example, Bank of England (2013a).

14. Transparency is not complete: notably, the regulator's own models are not published given the risk of gaming by the banks.

much-higher-than-planned equity capital requirement to banks (even 100 percent), that would simply lead to the problem of excess maturity transformation and leverage relocating elsewhere in the financial firmament.[15] Similarly, even if the payments part of commercial banking were *completely* separate, instability in wholesale markets, spilling into the wider economy, could occur from distress among trading intermediaries that were fragile and interconnected; "narrow banking" could not on its own make the world safe. Plus, history suggests that, more than other reforms, bans on activities are repealed by later generations. Hence the international community's "bookends' strategy": make financial institutions a lot more resilient but also make them resolvable without taxpayer solvency support.

Solving the TBTF problem is necessary to return banking to its place in market capitalism, and to stem creeping balkanization of global finance. There is no other way of solving the problem as only resolution policy engages directly with what happens when a firm faces *insolvency*.

In future, rather than focusing exclusively on the probability of failure, supervisors must also work backward from insolvency, ensuring that distress does not entail taxpayer bailout or a systemic crisis. This is already transforming how supervisors spend their time. But I have to say that the tens of thousands of pages churned out by banks for U.S. agencies in the name of "living wills" risk missing the big point, which is that groups must have simpler legal, financial, and organizational structures that positively enable orderly resolution. That is *the* big structural reform.[16] Regulators and resolution authorities must deliver it.

The model developed by the international community—putting losses exceeding equity onto bondholders and other creditors, regardless of geography but consistent with the creditor hierarchy—is essentially as follows.[17] Firms must be structured so that, either for the worldwide group as a whole or for well-defined subgroups, losses are transmitted upward to a group or intermediate holding company. And if that holding company is broken as a result, it is resolved by converting into equity

---

15. Larry Kotlikoff's (2010) proposal that all financial intermediaries be forcibly converted into mutual funds aims to be an intellectually coherent attempt to meet this point, but at the cost of garnering no practical support given the massive uncertainties of its effects.

16. This is not inconsistent with ring-fencing of *essential* services as a fallback.

17. See FSB (2013b).

FIGURE 4-3. Banks' Structure for the Future

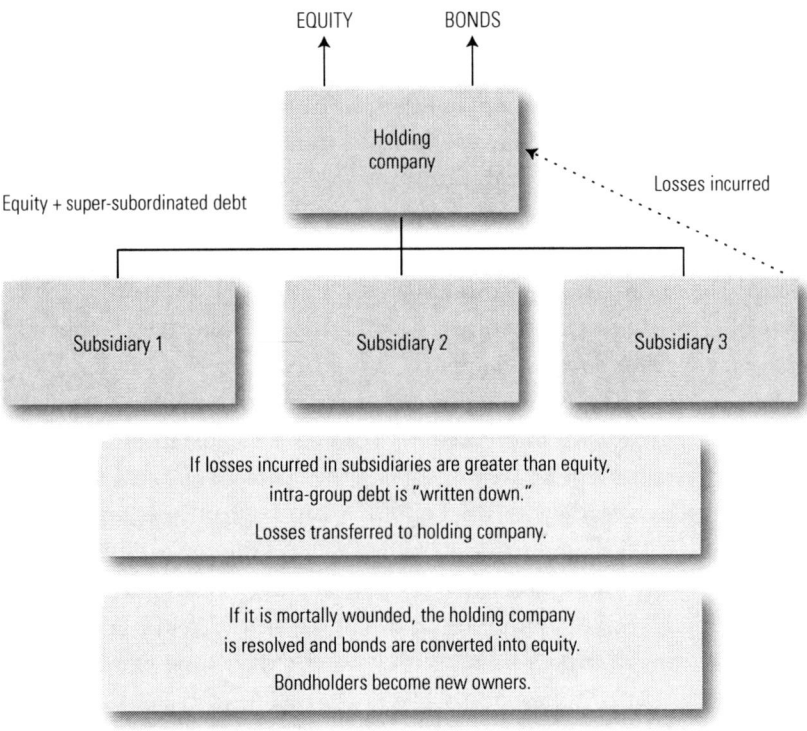

as much as necessary of externally issued bonds, whose holders become the new owners (see figure 4-3.) A plan for a group to be resolved as a whole is known as single-point-of-entry resolution. When a group is to be split up, it is multiple point of entry. Whether a financial group is subject to single or multiple point of entry—already widely referred to as SPE and MPE—will, I believe, transform the way banks are structured, run, and talked about over the coming decades. It should, for example, drive requirements on how equity capital is distributed across the entities in a group. The FDIC's plans for resolving U.S. SIFIs using its new Dodd-Frank powers fall firmly within this global model.

A necessary condition for it to work is that financial groups maintain in issue a critical mass of bonds that can be "bailed-in" to cover losses and recapitalize a firm to the required equity level. In my view, regulators should require group holding companies[18] to issue at least as much long-term debt as their equity requirement—that is, at least 10 percent of risk-weighted assets for the biggest groups, producing total loss-absorbing capacity (equity plus bonds) of over 20 percent *before* any operating liabilities would need to absorb losses. Last year's G-20 summit called on the Financial Stability Board to agree on a policy on this by this autumn.

These plans *can* solve the challenges in the cross-border resolution of international banking groups. In essence, the solution is for over-seas (and domestic) subsidiaries to issue supersubordinated debt to their parent group. This enables losses exceeding a subsidiary's equity to be transmitted up to the holding company, without the subsidiary itself going into default—at last making a reality of the long-standing doctrine, underpinning all consolidated supervision, that groups/sub-groups are a source of strength for their component parts.[19] If as a result the holding company is mortally wounded, the group's home country authorities can resolve it, and it alone. Thus a group-wide, global reso-lution is executed without operations across the planet going into local liquidation or resolution. Dodd-Frank legislation is entirely congruent with that. It is central to the recently finalized EU resolution legislation.

By framing the trigger for "converting" intragroup debt into equity, home and host authorities can hardwire cooperation; or if they fail to agree on a trigger, they will at least discover ex ante rather than ex post that they can't rely on each other. This would usefully give a harder edge to discussions among home and host authorities in supervisory and crisis-management colleges.[20]

Strengthened resolution regimes coupled with a restructuring of com-plex international groups can put the financial system on a more secure, market-based footing. If firms can be recapitalized via resolution, liquid-ity stress will be both slightly less likely, and, if it occurs, easier for

18. For multiple-point-of-entry groups, read: subgroup *intermediate* holding companies.

19. It is economically equivalent to a collateralized parental guarantee. A pure guarantee would leave a subsidiary and its host jurisdiction exposed to the ability and willingness of the holding company to pay.

20. The host authority for a key subsidiary must have a finger on the trigger for con-verting intragroup debt into equity. If the home country alone controlled the trigger, host authorities would likely be worried that the home authorities might not, in fact, pull the trigger. That would not help to stem regional balkanization of banking groups operating internationally.

the central banks to address, as discussed in the last section. By taking losses, bondholders' incentives can be flipped, making them active monitors of imprudence and so harnessing them to stability. The same goes for management if paid in debt that writes off to zero in resolution.

Important practical steps are needed over the next year or so to get over the finishing line, including eliminating cross-guarantees and other clauses that could trigger contracts being declared in default when a group is being resolved.[21] But it is now basically a matter of will. Those who doubt the willingness of the authorities to execute these plans in earnest should ask themselves what incentives officials face in again asking taxpayers, via governments and legislatures, to withstand a bust bank's losses.

Shadow Banking and Regulatory Arbitrage:
The Challenging Need for Regulatory Flexibility

The souped-up resolution regimes have to extend beyond banks to any institution that might endanger stability, not least because the business of banking will not stay wholly within firms treated by the law as banks. As banks are reregulated—with greater constraints on the structure of their balance sheets and on the types of asset they hold—the substance of banking will inevitably reemerge elsewhere: as shadow banking. Policymakers have therefore stressed the fragility of intermediaries heavily reliant on short-term wholesale funding, which frames the debate within the legitimate concerns of the lender of last resort.[22] Some of this is easy enough. Most obviously, don't let banking groups create, run, or stand behind off-balance vehicles that don't have to be consolidated for accounting or prudential purposes.[23] In a similar spirit, if an important institution is substantively a bank, regulate it as a bank—although, as I discuss later, this is easier said than done in some jurisdictions.

But it is more complicated than that. If TBTF is the single greatest challenge in underpinning financial stability, close behind it is endemic regulatory arbitrage. The financial services industry is a shape-shifter. As insurance firms have shown, with disastrous results in the case of the

---

21. See FSB (2013c).

22. This has been stressed by Governor Daniel Tarullo of the Federal Reserve Board. See, for example, proposition 4 in Tarullo (2013).

23. An interesting test will be whether, as they should, regulators require consolidation of constant-value money market mutual funds managed by banks' asset-management arms.

American International Group (AIG), anybody holding low-risk securities can build their own shadow bank by lending out ("repo-ing") their securities for cash and investing the proceeds in a riskier credit portfolio. That is, in principle, still amenable to the regulation of institutions. But *banking-like* fragility can be generated through Russian doll–like chains of transactions or structures via which *aggregate* leverage or liquidity mismatches, or both, to *gradually* accumulate, but that don't involve a financial firm that could be relabeled and regulated as a bank—an example in the run up to the crisis being conduits funded by short-term paper invested in tranches of securitizations themselves invested in securitized paper (figure 4-4). This broad phenomenon is an issue for emerging market economies as well as "advanced" economies.

Some good policies are in the pipeline.[24] Nevertheless, I worry that the authorities—perhaps particularly in the United States—face problems in finding robust solutions, partly for political economy reasons.

Legislators in many countries favor rules-based regulation in order to guard against the exercise of arbitrary power by unelected regulators. But a static rulebook is the meat and drink of regulatory arbitrage. And the more detailed the rules, the more rules arbitrage is implicitly legitimized, because the rulemakers must have said precisely what they meant and no more. "Reg-arb" is why money funds grew in the United States (Regulation Q), why asset-backed commercial paper conduits could be core to banks' treasury management unconstrained by bank regulation,[25] and quirks in regulation led to broker-dealer groups and commercial companies sidestepping bans on banking via so-called industrial banks in Utah *with* FDIC insurance. I could go on. This shape-shifting dynamic can leave policymakers in a game of catch-up, responding only as each incarnation becomes systemically significant—this year money funds, next year who knows what: real estate investment trusts, credit funds, leveraged exchange-traded funds? A game that sooner or later the authorities would be doomed to lose. That is not least because by the time the products of reg-arb are evidently systemically significant, they have the lobbying power to delay reform.

24. See FSB (2013a) and Tucker (2012).
25. U.S.-domiciled banks were active users of conduits and structured investment vehicles, making a canard of suggestions that the critical prudential failures were all in securities-dealer supervision and abroad.

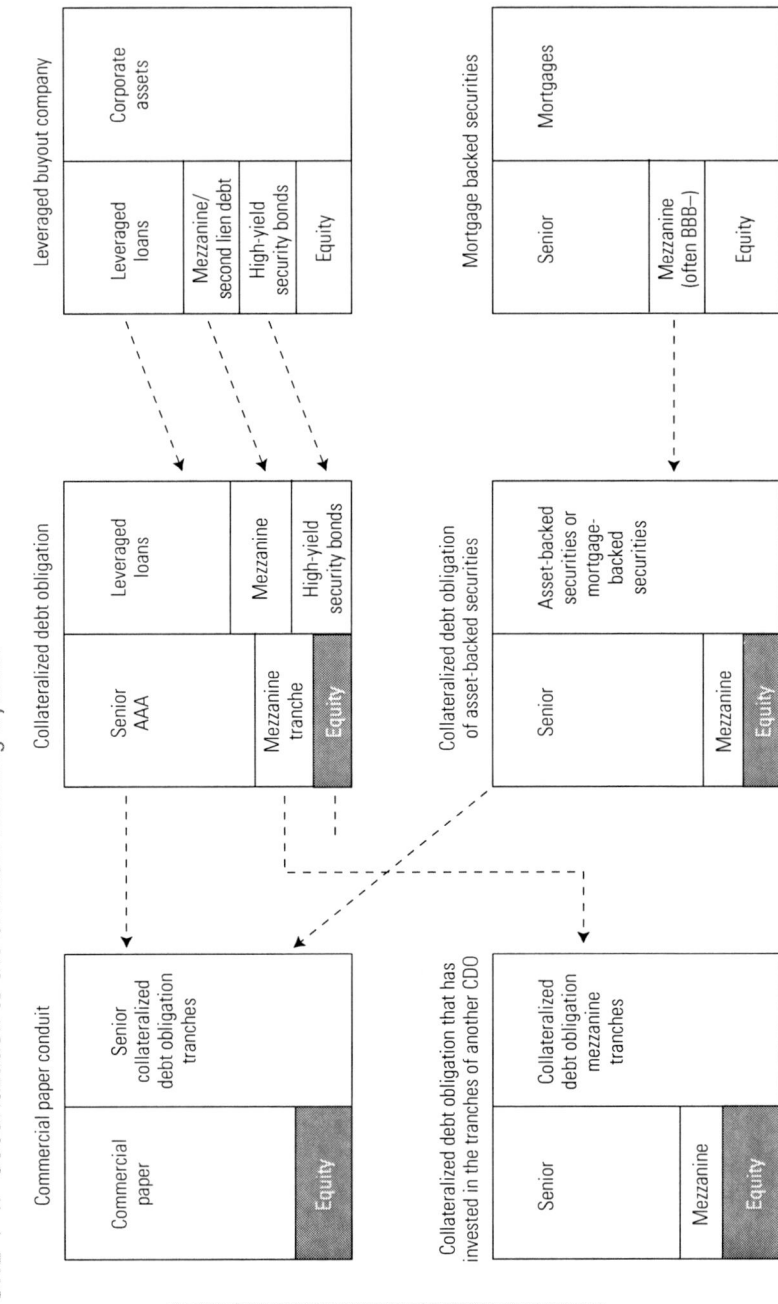

FIGURE 4-4. Securitization to the Shadow Banking System

Framing policies that are adaptable, legitimate, and consistent with the mandates of existing agencies would be a challenge. I return to this in discussing policy on markets and the importance of building new macroprudential regulatory institutions.

Central Counterparties:
Simplifying the Network and Residual Challenges

The fourth plank of policy is to simplify the network of credit exposures among banks and dealers. For their members, CCPs do this by acting as a buyer to every seller and a seller to every buyer in the markets they serve. By netting all offsetting transactions on a multilateral basis, they cancel bilateral exposures arising from transactions in the capital markets. And having absorbed the counterparty-credit risk onto itself, a CCP applies collateral (margin) requirements and holds a mutualized default fund in case its collateral falls short in the event of a member's default. In 2009 the G-20 leaders decided that all "standard OTC derivatives" must be cleared by CCPs. And to impede regulatory arbitrage, minimum margin requirements will be applied to remaining bilateral transactions. This is a coherent policy.

Nevertheless, three big issues were barely identified back in 2009: (1) What happens if a CCP fails? (2) Are they set up consistently with combining the social purpose of stability with the private purpose of generating profits for their owners? (3) Which markets should they clear?

Disorderly failure would cause mayhem. The benefits of simplifying the network of counterparty-credit exposures must be safeguarded by measures to ensure that CCPs redistribute post-netting risks back to their clearing members and, crucially, that they are resolvable without a taxpayer bailout. How tragic if they were too important to fail. Belatedly, the need for policies on the resolution of CCPs is in hand internationally and must not slip.[26] It is not clear which agency in the United States is gripping it.

---

26. The international standard is the principles for financial market infrastructure set forth by the Committee on Payment and Settlement Systems–International Organization of Securities Commissions (CPSS-IOSCO). CPSS-IOSCO is due to publish plans for loss-allocation recovery measures, and the FSB is due to make clear how the internationally agreed resolution regime would be applied to CCPs.

The challenge of combining private and social purposes may be more problematic. Increasingly part of vertically integrated exchange groups, clearinghouses are exposed to profit-making incentives that could distort their utility-like functions. They can and should act as system-risk monitors and managers in the markets they clear, with risk management policies that are not only among the best, but that take account of feedback effects and pro-cyclical dynamics. That requires a shift in mindset, which may be slow in coming absent well-targeted nudges from the authorities. Were a clearinghouse to fail in a disorderly way, I am certain that legislators would ask why on earth the authorities had allowed them to be for-profit entities.[27] But it does not appear that the issues around governance and incentives are being seized in the United States or elsewhere.

On the required scope of centrally cleared markets, it makes sense for derivatives to be centrally cleared, as in bilateral deals the buyers of protection are exposed to their "insurer's" ability to pay without being able to see its other exposures. Nevertheless, there is something distinctly odd about high-level policy having been cast in terms of only OTC contracts and derivatives. Why not cash instruments? Why not exchange-traded contracts? In fact, many cash instruments *are* being centrally cleared—both in the money markets (government bond repo) and exchange-traded securities (equities). Policy needs to pay as much attention to these activities, which present different liquidity risks, as to derivatives clearing. More widely, given the international reach of some infrastructure providers, and the certainty of cross-border spillovers if some others were to fail, there is as good a case for applying special policies to *globally systemic infrastructure providers* as to global banks.

BANKING MEETS CAPITAL MARKETS: GAPS IN THE REFORM PROGRAM

The foregoing brief survey of the four planks of the core reform program indicates that two of them in particular—CCPs and shadow banking—bridge banking policy and markets policy. But there is more to

---

27. For similar sentiments, see Dudley (2013). William C. Dudley is the president of the New York Federal Reserve Bank.

do given changes over the past forty years or so. Once upon a time, banks extended and held illiquid loans, overseen by banking supervisors. And in a largely separate universe, securities regulators policed the integrity of *individual* transactions and offerings of securities on *public* exchanges served by specialist broking and market-making intermediaries. That world is long gone. The terrain has been transformed by the growth of *private* capital markets, trading of loans, OTC markets, derivatives, securitization of portfolios of illiquid assets, and short-term money (or repo) markets employing a vast range of securities as collateral. Further, with controls on cross-border flows of capital having been dismantled more than a generation ago, most markets are international. Absent a seismic shift in global politics, there is no chance of the clock being completely turned back.

This matters for stability, as illustrated by the example of securities lending being used to "roll your own shadow bank." It isn't enough to focus on large systemic institutions, or on banks more generally. Activities and markets matter for stability too. During 2007, liquidity in markets for borrowing secured against asset-backed securities (ABS-repo) evaporated when credit-rating agency (CRA) ratings were called into question. Traders relying on what had seemed a deep secured-financing market were left high and dry. Problems in the underlying capital markets were compounded. Lesson: a *money market* becoming big can do great damage if it turns out to have flakey foundations.

More generally, prices in the *underlying asset markets* don't always self-correct in orderly ways. Imagine a market in which pretty much all of the demand turns out to be from levered investors; the most senior tranches of ABS might be an example. In buoyant states of the world, the market would be prone to elevated valuations, making the asset class uneconomic for unlevered investors. But if the risks in the instruments haven't been grasped and overissuance makes them more risky still, the dominant levered investors will rush for the door when they are shaken out of their myopia.[28] A sharp correction might drive the cost of finance for *new* issues to prohibitive levels, tightening credit conditions if there aren't ready alternative sources. Such fire sales can constitute instability with social costs.

28. See Gennaioli, Shleifer, and Vishny (2010).

If this is correct, there are worrying signs of policy malaise. First, there is *faltering vigor* in pursuing some intended market reforms, as is evident in

—The lack of convergence in accounting standards, and in the United States a strong *Financial Accounting Standards Board* commitment to mark to market even longish-term investments.

—The persistence internationally of official sector policies, and hence private sector investment practices, mechanistically linked to CRA ratings, contrary to a G-20 decision over three years ago.[29]

—The project to develop trade repositories having to be forcibly steered back to the G-20 objective of making it easier for macroprudential authorities to see how the financial system fits together.

—Still not having much information on the leverage of hedge funds to help understand vulnerabilities in the financial system, notwithstanding the 2009 G-20 summit declaration making this a priority.[30]

Second, *clarity of purpose and coherence* seem somewhat lacking. That is suggested by the uncertainty around whether the cocktail of banking/insurance/securities/accounting reforms have cleaned up securitization markets or overshot, impeding markets that indirectly give small borrowers access to the capital markets. Similarly, it seems to be difficult to find agreed high-level objectives to help adjudicate between U.S., EU, and Asian securities regulators on whether policies on trading platforms and transparency should apply across borders.

A Missing Framework for Markets Policy

These are symptoms of a missing conceptual framework for stability policy on markets. There isn't an off-the-shelf equivalent of figure 4-1.

Such a framework would need to address the big question of which markets are especially important to the real economy, or to the financial system itself, and what qualities those markets need to avoid egregious risks to stability. Key concepts would be, respectively, whether there were ready substitutes if a market closed, and the *resilience* of the liquidity of a *systemically relevant* market. A framework of that kind

---

29. See FSB (2010). In the United States the problem is different: an absolute ban on regulators placing any weight on CRA ratings.

30. See, for example, Bank of England (2013b). The desire for the information does not reflect a view that the fund industry is necessarily systemic.

FIGURE 4-5. Linking the Spheres

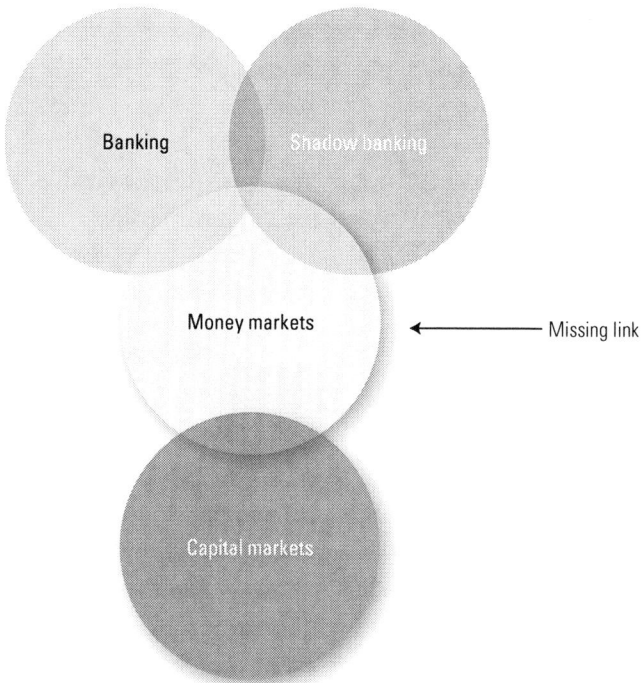

would have focused policymakers' attention on the workings of the ABS markets and, in particular, on the associated repo markets well before the crisis. It might also help to design reforms to property finance, and to decide whether or not there could be meaningful threats to stability from, for example, asset-management practices and structures,[31] dark pools, and algorithmic trading.

On market liquidity, the authorities need to examine not only risks in the underlying instruments individually—the traditional approach of listing authorities—but also any risks associated with heavy *aggregate* issuance and the associated indebtedness of the underlying borrower *class*. As those underlying risks build, the capital market might be put in jeopardy directly, or indirectly if the associated secured-financing market

31. The U.S. Treasury's Office of Financial Research (2013) has published a paper on possible implications of concentrations in asset management.

has become unsustainably big. Like any money market, a repo market will be liquid only if the participants believe they don't need to examine each collateral bundle.[32] Money markets are the key link between banking and shadow banking, and the capital markets (figure 4-5).

Policy Instruments

This approach suggests a range of policy measures for *systemically relevant markets,* distinguishing between the capital market and its associated financing market(s). For example, infrastructure could be prescribed, settlement periods could be shorter, the dealer community could be stronger, circuit-breakers could be contemplated, CRA practices could be overhauled, warnings could be issued about risks given aggregate patterns of issuance, and for the secured-financing markets in particular, minimum collateral requirements could be set or raised.

While some of those instruments would be novel—such as a new macroprudential approach to the functions of the listing authority—others are already more or less incorporated into the international reform program. The most important instance of that is the plan to set minimum requirements on the haircuts (that is, the excess collateral) taken in repo and securities-lending transactions.[33] This is warranted because, as with bank capital levels, left to themselves private markets will tend to set haircuts that are too low given the social costs of uncovered defaults; and also because haircuts have been pro-cyclical, being shaved as markets become more buoyant, less volatile, and apparently liquid, only to be raised sharply when conditions deteriorate.[34] In economic substance, such minimum requirements are akin to a cap on the leverage of the counterparties (if that is their main source of finance), so can give the authorities indirect levers over some variants of shadow banking. They need to be paired with minimum overcollateralization requirements for credit

---

32. The importance of information-insensitive securities, epitomized by money-market instruments, is stressed in a series of papers by Gary Gorton and Bengt Holmström. See, for example, Holmström (2008). Some central banks examined ABS collateral bundles very carefully when, as ABS-repo dried up during the crisis, they widened the instruments eligible in their liquidity-insurance operations to support banking-system liquidity and funding.

33. Parallel requirements will be set on the initial margin (up-front collateral) taken in derivatives transactions, whether centrally cleared or otherwise. They will need to be consistent because derivatives can be structured to synthesize financing transactions.

34. For the increase in repo haircuts during the crisis, see Gorton and Metrick (2009).

vehicles funded in short-term commercial paper markets, which mimics a bank capital requirement. This illustrates the need for consistent policy across the fuzzy boundaries between markets, vehicles, and firms.

But where the underlying collateral is fundamentally unsuitable for a *money* market, the authorities might need to go farther. If spotted in time, this might mean impeding the development of a money market, offsetting the inducements of overgenerous CRA ratings, and insisting on maximum transparency to underpin the policy. Where the authorities are late but still ahead of the markets, a richer response is needed so that the authorities don't bring about the crisis they aim to prevent. This underlines the need to think about markets policy in a new way.

BUILDING INSTITUTIONS:
A NEW REGULATORY ARCHITECTURE AND CULTURE

The reforms under way in banking, those needed in market regulation, and wider lessons about regulatory arbitrage and macroeconomic-financial system feedback mechanisms necessitate institutional and cultural change among regulatory agencies. Above all, central banks and banking supervisors are having to recover their historic mission for systemic stability.

Implications for Securities Regulators

The implications for securities regulators are equally momentous. Typically, securities regulators have micro-regulatory jurisdiction over capital markets, asset managers, and many manifestations of shadow banking. But their statutory objectives and historical mission and cultures are centered on the vital importance of honesty and efficiency in the interests of investor protection, rather than on avoiding runs and, more broadly, preserving systemic stability. Given the changes in markets over recent decades, securities regulators have to grow beyond their roots. And they need to invest more in agreeing on common policies internationally via the International Organization of Securities Commissions (IOSCO). But this is not easy. International agreements entail openness and compromise. In the United States, protracted debate about money market mutual fund reform, notwithstanding the domestic and international macroprudential consensus, has left the rest of the world anxious about the capacity of the authorities here to grapple with shadow banking. In the United Kingdom, people worry that the Financial Conduct Authority will not give sufficient weight to its prudential oversight of funds and asset managers or to using its listing-authority powers in the interests of stability. Some reorientation of securities regulators' objectives and priorities toward stability is needed.[35] It is the responsibility of legislatures to help that happen, through legislation and questions asked during testimony.

But central banks and banking supervisors need to meet securities regulators halfway, widening their engagement on markets and finance. "Macropru" is a lot more than banking supervision for macroeconomists. Among other things, central banks should accept that standing at the apex of the monetary system, they have a special responsibility for the health of the money markets.

Overlap is preferable to underlap: turf disputes won't work as a defense for failing the public. The creation of macroprudential authorities is the big initiative intended to address these issues.

Macroprudential Institutions: Flexibility Redux

Preserving stability without sacrificing efficiency requires policies that are highly adaptable to innovations, regulatory arbitrage, and evolving cyclical conditions. Flexibility is needed to avoid overregulation and the stability of the graveyard; we need healthy market-based finance. Policy must be joined up across sectors. But diversity is also badly needed. The authorities need instrument independence in order to overcome the time-consistency problem of credibly committing to "take away the punchbowl," building resilience to mitigate threats from incipient booms. That package can't be achieved unless legislators give macroprudential authorities appropriate goals, powers and discretions, for which they can be held accountable.

In the United States, the umbrella macroprudential body is the Financial Stability Oversight Council (FSOC). Its design is, perhaps, imperfect. It is a committee of representatives, whose duties to Congress relate to

---

35. The new Principle 6 of IOSCO's core principles calls upon jurisdictions to give securities regulators a stability objective ranking equally with other objectives, but implementation is at best patchy. Note that I designed a securities regulatory system some years ago (in Hong Kong).

the agencies they head rather than the FSOC's stability objective.[36] Where it has clear powers, its authority has already been apparent: notably, in designating some non-banks as "systemically important." As well as Federal Reserve oversight, that entails submitting annually to the FDIC a plan for how they might be resolved *under regular bankruptcy law* without destabilizing the U.S. financial system, an essay question it will be hard to pass. But quite apart from the hazards in the label, the new U.S. regulatory regime does not cater well for circumstances where no *individual* non-bank of a particular kind is "systemic"; taken together, however, a group of medium-sized firms or funds, or an activity, could bring about systemic distress. It is not yet clear how much force the FSOC's public recommendations to the various regulatory agencies will carry. That is the essence of the money market mutual fund problem.

The other dimension of macroprudential policy is building resilience during booms. While U.S. legislators did not explicitly address "cyclical" variations of regulatory requirements in the Dodd-Frank Act, the Federal Reserve probably has discretion to make temporary changes to banks' headline capital requirements. It is less clear which U.S. agency could and would be prepared to vary minimum margin/haircut requirements.

Added to that, international cooperation may be needed. No country can combine open capital markets and cross-border banking, financial stability, and autonomy in national policy.[37] At the least, home and host authorities will need to coordinate on setting countercyclical buffers for internationally active banks. More widely, some national measures may be taken to mitigate threats to stability from unaddressed flaws in the international monetary system. For example, the cross-border, cross-currency carry trade remains as potent as ever, leaving some countries concerned about volatile capital flows associated with burgeoning short-term external liabilities. Employing macroprudential instruments to influence the *composition* of inflows and so mitigate vulnerabilities in national balance sheets may sometimes make sense but entails a degree of collective surveillance of the global system.[38]

---

36. The United Kingdom's Financial Policy Committee is different in that respect.

37. On the *financial stability trilemma*, see Schoenmaker (2013).

38. This might well have been a more fruitful way into postcrisis debates about the international monetary and financial system than the focus on symmetric adjustment of cumulative current account imbalances.

In terms of building institutions, it is unclear whether the FSOC, supported by the Office of Financial Research, can handle all those dimensions of macroprudential policy. What happens when a source of risk is not within the current jurisdiction of *any* micro-regulator? Whatever the answers, the Federal Reserve needs to be ready to take to the FSOC table, and make public, its views on what actions other U.S. agencies should take to preserve stability. Even where responsibility for supervisory lapses lies elsewhere, the consequences can end up at the central bank's door—or, rather, on its balance sheet.

Implications for the Lender of Last Resort

As institutions created in order to ensure the stability of the monetary system, central banks have been in crisis too. Relying on monetary policy to mop up proved deeply flawed when the backbone of the credit system collapsed. Moreover, actions taken to contain the early stages of crisis met with a mixed reception. As well as providing lender-of-last-resort assistance to depository institutions, central banks have acted as marketmakers of last resort, as LOLR to non-banks, and even, through soft terms, arguably as capital-of-last-resort providers in some cases.[39] However vital in containing instability, those operations raised questions of legitimacy.[40] The regulatory reforms help to address those concerns.

Some of the challenges are old and revolve around forbearance. The time that the central bank provides to banks and the economy more widely to address underlying problems may not be used well. Central banks that are also prudential supervisors can be tempted to lend to fundamentally unsound firms, in the hope that something will turn up to cover their supervisory failures. And having provided assistance, they may be tempted to extend support beyond the point at which the firm is clearly insolvent.

The reforms *can* make a big difference. Systematic, transparent stress testing should make it much harder for supervisors to avoid facing up to a firm's problems being fundamentally of solvency. And if a firm deteriorates *after* liquidity assistance has been provided, with a forthcoming stress test set to reveal the problem has become solvency, central banks

---

39. See, for example, Humphrey (2010).
40. See Goodfriend (2013).

should no longer face a desperate choice between maintaining support or pulling the plug. The firm can go into resolution. With termination of lending credible, there will be stronger incentives for borrowers to use the time provided by LOLR support. All this should help to underpin the operational independence of central banks and other supervisors, shielding them from the day-to-day political interventions that would be hard to avoid if the only credible backstop were a taxpayer bailout of bondholders and other uninsured creditors. In addition, post-resolution provision of liquidity assistance should be a more powerful signal that solvency and basic viability have been restored.[41]

A second set of issues revolves around scope. What if destructive fire sales can be contained only by providing liquidity to solvent non-bank financial institutions or by acting as a backstop marketmaker? That is partly about finding a time-consistent policy, which lies beyond the scope of this discussion.[42] But it is also about jurisdictions facing up to intermediaries regulated as non-banks in fact conducting banking. Before the crisis, an obvious case was the U.S. securities dealers. They suffered a massive liquidity run when hedge funds and others withdrew idle balances on demand. Prime brokerage services included basic banking. Is the system any better now at proactively confronting such regulatory anomalies?

SUMMING UP: STATIC RULES VERSUS FLEXIBILITY

To reiterate, the crisis left the credibility of supervisors and regulators in tatters. It won't be repaired quickly.

A problem in assessing improvements in *supervision* is that it is mighty difficult to spot bad supervision from the outside. In assessing a modern monetary policy regime, pretty well everything is written on the tin: the objective, the instruments, and the models, but also the deliberations of the policymakers. What society gets is what it sees. Contrast that with prudential supervision. The regulatory laws, rulebooks, and published policies might all look fine but give a misleading picture of

---

41. U.S. legislation permits the Federal Reserve to lend secured on a bilateral basis to banking businesses being returned to viability via resolution, and to lend to non-banks in similar circumstances via market-wide facilities.

42. See Tucker (2009) for some principles for market maker of last resort operations.

the reality of supervision on the ground. That is one reason why the International Monetary Fund's assessments of countries' regimes failed to expose deeply flawed supervisory practices before the crisis. It is why a shift in transparency is needed, and why the advent of systematic stress testing is so important. Even then, there's a question of how to keep the supervisors on the straight and narrow. I would like to see multinational teams—drawn from key hosts as well as the home supervisors—involved in *collective* stress testing of the global SIFIs, including central counterparties.

In contrast to supervision, it is easier to see what is really going on with overhauling *regulation*. But a distinction needs to be made between banking and capital markets. The core program for reforming banking is coherent: reduce leverage, opacity, and interconnectedness; improve liquidity; and transform resolvability. Whether it does the job depends above all on two conditions. First, will all firms truly be resolvable without taxpayer solvency support: bail-in, not bailout? Solving the TBTF problem is definitely within reach: it is now a matter of will. It can help to put a brake on the balkanization of international finance by providing a framework for determining the distribution of equity capital across a group, and by hardwiring cooperation between home and host authorities. In addition to the Financial Stability Board's peer-review process, which *must* involve truly top officials who will be on the line when a firm fails, enough information must also be made public for third parties to judge resolvability. I am more agnostic about the second precondition for success: whether the authorities will be sufficiently fleet of foot and the regime sufficiently *flexible* to keep up with regulatory arbitrage driving the substance of banking into shadow banks. The 2013 summit concluded that all jurisdictions must have a regime for coping with threats to stability from shadow banking. The jury on whether this will be delivered is out. Some jurisdictions have done more than others.[43]

The story on the markets is somewhat less compelling. There is less coherence, faltering vigor, and conflicting views about how different national regimes should apply to inherently international markets.

43. For example, in the United Kingdom Parliament has established that on the recommendation of the Bank of England's Financial Policy Committee, the perimeter of regulation may be changed by the executive government subject to expedited review by Parliament itself (secondary legislation).

Arguably there is also more time, but not much. Jurisdictions need to enrich the statutory objectives of their securities regulators, or endow macroprudential authorities with wide and *flexible powers* to take action to forestall threats to stability—whether structural or cyclical—from anywhere in the financial system.

I have stressed *flexibility* rather than a static rulebook. Coping with endemic regulatory arbitrage and the shape-shifting dynamic of finance requires that. Similarly, to be sufficiently forward-looking to mitigate serious threats from the credit cycle, the authorities will need degrees of freedom (instrument independence) hitherto more familiar in monetary policy than in regulation. This raises real political economy issues, perhaps especially in the United States, owing to the need either for greater discretion to be granted to regulatory agencies or for a more expeditious legislative process. The challenge is to establish a regime of *constrained discretion*, as advanced in the monetary policy sphere. There seems to have been more debate about this in Europe, including in the United Kingdom, where the new statutory regime is explicitly macroprudential. That being so, if only to protect its balance sheet and reputation, the Federal Reserve will need to be noisy when it sees real threats to stability, whatever turf it crosses.

But to conclude on a positive note, some of the problems presented by LOLR operations can be cured by the regulatory reforms, particularly the development of improved resolution technology and of systematic, transparent stress testing. This is of first-order importance and owes much to thinking in the Federal Reserve under Chairman Bernanke. Central bankers need to keep their LOLR role, and therefore the adequacy of the regulatory regime, at the heart of their principles and practices. If they do, the world won't be completely safe, but it will be safer.

REFERENCES

Adrian, Tobias, and Hyun Song Shin. 2010. "Liquidity and Leverage." *Journal of Financial Intermediation* 19 (3): 418–37.

Aghion, Philippe, and Enisse Kharroubi. 2013. "Cyclical Macroeconomic Policy, Financial Regulation and Economic Growth." Working Paper 434. Basel, Switzerlaqnd: Bank for International Settlements (December).

Bank of England. July 2006. "Financial Stability Review." Issue 20 (www. bankofengland.co.uk/publications/Documents/fsr/2006/fsrfull0606.pdf).

————. 2013a. "A Framework for Stress Testing the UK Banking System." Bank of England discussion paper (October) (www.bankofengland.co.uk/financial stability/fsc/Documents/discussionpaper1013.pdf).

————. June 2013b. "Financial Stability Report." Issue 33 (www.bankofengland. co.uk/publications/Documents/fsr/2013/fsrfull1306.pdf).

Dudley, William C. 2013. Remarks at Panel Discussion on OTC Derivatives Reform and Broader Financial Reforms Agenda. Banque de France conference, Paris (www.newyorkfed.org/newsevents/speeches/2013/dud130912.html).

Duffie, Darrell. 2013. "The Leverage Ratio and Bank Capital Requirements: Presentation on the Limitations of a Leverage Limit." Brookings Conference, October 31 (www.brookings.edu/events/2013/10/31-leverage-ratio-bank-capital-requirements).

Financial Stability Board (FSB). 2010. "Principles for Reducing Reliance on CRA Ratings" (www.financialstabilityboard.org/publications/r_101027.pdf).

————. 2013a. "An Overview of Policy Recommendations on Shadow Banking" (August) (www.financialstabilityboard.org/publications/r_130829a.htm).

————. 2013b. "Guidance on Developing Effective Resolution Strategies" (July). (www.financialstabilityboard.org/publications/r_130716b.htm).

————. 2013c. "Report to the G20: Progress and Next Steps Towards Ending 'Too-Big-To-Fail' (TBTF)" (September) (www.financialstabilityboard.org/publications/r_130902.pdf).

————. 2013d. "To G20 Leaders: Progress of Financial Reforms" (September 5) (www.financialstabilityboard.org/publications/r_130905.pdf).

Financial Stability Forum. 2000. "Report of the Working Group on Capital Flows: Meeting of the Financial Stability Forum" (www.financialstability board.org/publications/r_0004.pdf).

————. 2001. "Joint G10/Financial Stability Forum Report." Unpublished.

Gennaioli, Nicola, Andrei Shleifer, and Robert W. Vishny. 2010. "Neglected Risks, Financial Innovation, and Financial Fragility." Working Paper 16068. Cambridge, Mass.: National Bureau of Economic Research (June) (www.nber. org/papers/w16068).

Goodfriend, Marvin. 2013. "The Elusive Promise of Independent Central Banking" (http://ideas.repec.org/p/ime/imedps/12-e-09.html).

Gorton, Gary, and Andrew Metrick. 2009. "Securitized Banking and the Run on Repo" (http://ideas.repec.org/a/eee/jfinec/v104y2012i3p425-451.html).

Holmström, Bengt. 2008. "Commentary: The Panic of 2007. Comment on a Paper by Gorton." Jackson Hole (www.kc.frb.org/publicat/sympos/2008/Holmstrom. 03.12.09.pdf).

Humphrey, Thomas M. 2010. "Lender of Last Resort: What It Is, Whence It Came, and Why the Fed Isn't It." *Cato Journal* 30 (2) (http://citeseerx.ist.psu. edu/viewdoc/download?doi=10.1.1.165.5749&rep=rep1&type=pdf).

Kayshap, Anil K., Raghuram Rajan, and Jeremy C. Stein. 2002. "Banks as Liquidity Providers: Explaining the Co-Existence of Lending and Deposit-Taking." *Journal of Finance* 57 (1): 33–73.

Kotlikoff, Laurence J. 2010. *Jimmy Stewart Is Dead: Ending the World's Ongoing Financial Plague with Limited Purpose Banking.* Hoboken, N.J.: John Wiley & Sons.

Schoenmaker, Dirk. 2013. *Governance of International Banking: The Financial Trilemma*. Oxford University Press.

Tarullo, Daniel K. 2013. "Macroprudential Regulation." Speech at the Yale Law School conference, "Challenges in Global Financial Services," New Haven, Conn., September 20 (www.federalreserve.gov/newsevents/speech/tarullo 20130920a.htm).

Tucker, Paul. 2009. "The Repertoire of Official Sector Interventions in the Financial System: Last Resort Lending, Market-Making, and Capital." Speech at the international conference, "Financial System and Monetary Policy Implementation," Bank of Japan, May 27–28 (www.bankofengland.co.uk/archive/Documents/historicpubs/speeches/2009/speech390.pdf).

———. 2012. "Shadow Banking: Thoughts for a Possible Policy Agenda" (April) (www.bis.org/review/r120427a.pdf).

———. 2013. "Resolution and the Future of Finance" (May) (www.bis.org/review/r130606a.pdf).

U.S. Treasury, Office of Financial Research. 2013. "Asset Management and Financial Stability" (September) (www.treasury.gov/initiatives/ofr/research/Documents/OFR_AMFS_FINAL.pdf).

DISCUSSION

Rodgin Cohen of Sullivan & Cromwell, a prominent banking lawyer, responded to Paul Tucker's presentation, focusing on changes in the regulatory architecture designed to limit the risks of taxpayer bailouts of big banks. David Wessel then moderated a wide-ranging discussion with other panelists and the audience.

COHEN: I'm going to focus on two fundamental points raised by Paul's thoughtful, comprehensive, and provocative remarks.

First, it is undeniable that the risk of failure of a major bank must be sharply reduced from what it was in 2008 by reform of the regulatory system, and that the systemic consequences that could result from such a failure must be dealt with by a credible and effective resolution regime. But as Paul writes, "The banking package of reforms is coherent and well-conceived, seeking to address the deep-seated flaws in our banks and regulatory system, including the biggest of all, too-big-to-fail."

In other words, although there is still much to do, we are generally on the right track. Calls for more radical reform of not just the regulatory system but the basic structure of the banking system are both unnecessary and fraught with their own risk. As Paul later notes, narrow banking could not, on its own, make the world safe. Indeed, I would suggest that reducing bank geographic and business diversification, and to Paul's earlier point, pushing financial activities into the shadow-banking sector, could have exactly the opposite effect.

Second and relatedly, Paul makes the crucial point, "Solving too-big-to-fail matters hugely because improvements in bank regulation and supervision alone will not confine the stress to the dustbin." There are two aspects of placing too-big-to-fail into its own dustbin. The first is moral hazard, which is dealt with directly by the Dodd-Frank legislation in mandating that creditors as well as stockholders bear all losses in the event of a failure.

The second is a resolution regime that can minimize the risk of serious systemic consequences. As Paul mentioned, essential to his approach for developing such a regime is a combination of long-term debt at the holding-company level and internal debt at the operating-subsidiary level, what is sometimes known as prepositioning. In the event of catastrophic losses, the banking organizations' equity would absorb the losses, and the debt would become equity to provide a cushion for recapitalization.

Let me discuss three issues quickly. The first is *how much*. At the holding-company level, I agree with Paul's view that the amount should generally be around 10 percent of risk-weighted assets for more complex institutions, assuming an equivalent amount of equity. You can site historical examples of institutions that have encountered even greater losses, but the long-term debt requirement should be calibrated to a reasonable worst-case scenario in today's regulatory environment rather than to the worst result ever.

However, if there is to be prepositioning, the amount of internal debt required at the operating-subsidiary level should be based on a lower percentage of risk-weighted assets, perhaps 5 percent. The principle reason is flexibility. In the event that an operating subsidiary experiences losses greater than its equity, as unlikely as that might be, the holding company would then have a reserve of recapitalization assets to fill the hole after utilizing the prepositioned debt. In addition, I worry that a higher requirement will encourage ring-fencing, which is antithetical to the type of resolution structure that Paul supports.

The second issue is related to the conditions for pulling the debt into equity trigger. In my view, triggers should not be hair triggers. The regulators need discretion, but it should be limited. I would recommend a typical insolvency test—inability to pay debts as they become due. If we have a specific capital-depletion trigger, it should be at a level where any private sector recapitalization is improbable.

I recommend this approach because once the trigger is pulled, the life of the banking institution is likely to be measured in days, if not hours. Funders and counterparties will flee, and once one host country pulls the trigger, it will be difficult for others to resist. If a major bank is prematurely placed in resolution proceeding, the world's financial system will be plunged into uncertainty. I accept the too-late concern, but this should be allayed by the substantial debt shield that Paul proposes.

There is a special issue relating to host-country discretion. Paul suggests that the host country must have a hand on the trigger because otherwise "host authorities would likely be worried that the home authorities might not, in fact, pull the trigger." I would suggest perhaps the option of adopting obligations for action at the parent level, as opposed to placing too many hands on what is a truly nuclear trigger.

The third and last issue created by Paul's proposal is how will the resolution regime be established and implemented on an international basis? As a general principle, the more binding the international arrangements are, the greater the certainty that the regime will be implemented as intended. This principle will, however, need to be applied in the context of political reality. It could be best effectuated, I believe, by binding treaties. If that is not feasible, as Paul suggests, there should be a formal written document endorsed by the regulators, the central banks, and ideally the Group of 20 heads of state or finance ministers.

One other possible approach is a series of understandings among the key regulators. In my view this is an inferior option as the market may assume that it is not worth the paper it is not written on.

As Paul says, solving the too-big-to-fail problem is definitely within reach. It is now a matter of will. And I'd like to note that as Chairman Ben Bernanke so vividly demonstrated, where there is a will and courage of conviction, there is a way.

WESSEL: Is there a risk that this all sounds good, but we're (a) going too far in constraining credit, or (b) making something so complicated that there's no chance it will ever work?

COHEN: I actually think the package of reforms today is a relatively reasonable reform. What concerns me, and I wish someone—maybe it's Brookings or the Financial Stability Oversight Council—would actually study everything that is being done on a holistic basis before you can determine your very critical question of whether there's going to be a constraint on credit. I do worry that the interaction of so many of these could produce a constraint, even though no one proposal or no one reform is doing so.

TUCKER: I basically agree with that. Something that may not have been studied very much in this country is Europe's Liikanen Report.[44] Whatever one thinks about its conclusions on structure, the first two-thirds of the report provide a pretty careful study of all the different regulatory measures in a joined-up way.

---

44. See http://ec.europa.eu/internal_market/bank/docs/high-level_expert_group/report_en.pdf.

WESSEL: Would you talk a bit more about your concern that financial reform hasn't gone far enough in the non-bank piece of the financial system?

TUCKER: The problem with the non-bank piece, or the market's part of this, is the lack of conceptual framework. Banking policies, for good or ill, are clearly informed by a sense that the problems were excess leverage, excess opacity, excess interconnectedness, excess maturity mismatch, and too-big-to-fail. Behind each of those things lies a body of analysis and economic research. There is no equivalent framework for thinking about markets policy. The most important point for policymakers is that they badly need a framework for the markets policy, and it has to be something to do with trying to identify which markets are systemically relevant because the economy or financial system depends so heavily on them, and whether the liquidity of those markets is illusory or resilient.

What we saw in the asset-backed securities market and, in particular, the associated secured money market was that everyone behaved as though these asset-backed securities were information insensitive and completely safe. Actually, they flipped to be highly information sensitive almost as soon as something went wrong.

That could have been foreseen if policymakers, analysts, and economists had had a framework for thinking about the resilience of markets as well as a framework for thinking about the resilience of firms. And I do think this is on the way.

JOHN WILLIAMS: Paul talked a lot about convertible debt and addressing too-big-to-fail. The concern I always have is with these trigger points. Once people start worrying that this trigger may be pulled, financial markets won't wait around to find out. They're going to run, or potentially could run, and whenever I hear a discussion about convertible debt I immediately think about this.

TUCKER: This is a very Federal Reserve point of view. The Federal Reserve thinks that all the problems are liquidity problems. And the liquidity problems are curable if you can sort out the solvency of the institution.

WILLIAMS: What is wrong with just having more equity? Anat Admati and her coauthors have been pleading for the past couple of years to just hold more equity.[45] Don't make it complicated; don't make it too sophisticated, just more equity.

---

45. See www.econstor.eu/bitstream/10419/57505/1/636811883.pdf.

TUCKER: That's a good point, but it hasn't happened. And neither the Federal Reserve nor the Bank of England has argued for more equity. You can take what I'm describing as second best if you like, but conditional on the current policy on equity. Then what's to be done? And this isn't convertible equity in the sense of a convertible bond. This is regular senior bonded debt, which, as Rodgin describes, could be flipped into being equity at the discretion of the authorities.

Rodgin raises a profoundly important point about the bankruptcy trigger, and mine is very similar. Essentially, the authorities should not have the power to do this unless the institution otherwise fulfilled the criteria for going into resolutional bankruptcy.

MARTIN FELDSTEIN: There is a big difference between equity and potentially convertible debt in terms of the cost of the funds to the bank and ultimately to its customers. It's cheaper to do the bonds, which have a certain probability of turning into equity but are not full-scale equity. I've always been attracted to the idea of having this extra class of security that is debt that can be converted to equity when there is a critical moment where more equity is needed, rather than having straight-out higher equity ratios.

PAUL SALTZMAN (president of The Clearing House): Is there a tension between the integrity associated with stress testing and concerns that stress testing as it's currently envisioned is a little opaque? The modeling is opaque and not transparent, and the assumptions are somewhat subjective. How do you reconcile those tensions with the effectiveness of stress testing?

WILLIAMS: I think stress testing is the most important transformative change in our supervisory approach. Is it opaque? We've tried pretty hard to make it more transparent. Are there subjective assumptions? Yes. You're going to come up with scenarios that are based on some analysis of things, but it's awfully hard to say this is the appropriate way exactly to model that.

One of the important cultural changes that we've seen in the Federal Reserve is that economists, regulators, and supervisors actually talk to each other and work together to think about these issues. Now in the Federal Reserve, we're using our economists to do risk modeling and analysis that's used in a supervisory process, and the economists have learned the importance of the supervisory approach too. Yes, there are issues with the subjectivity of assumptions. There's a lot of research going on at the Federal Reserve that is quite intriguing about how to properly frame the question of how to do stress testing and how to analyze this and think about that. It's an area with a lot of research, but it's been a fundamental change and a positive change.

FELDSTEIN: The stress testing is a very good thing. On the other hand, when you think how large and complex financial institutions are, and you think what would happen in case of economic weakness or a replay of the events of 2007, it's hard to have any confidence in the outcome of those stress tests. It's got to get better over time, but it's a little frightening in terms of depending upon it. And then if you think about the application of this in the euro zone, there are lots of doubts about whether stress testing is being done in a fair, honest, and open way with respect to all of the countries.

WESSEL: I thought that the issue was that the banks want to tell us what we need to do and we'll do those things. And the Fed is saying we don't want to do it that way because you'll just game the system. Are the stress tests being done well?

COHEN: In the United States they are definitely being done well. If you can just imagine how much time boards of directors alone are spending on reviewing those stress tests.

But it is very difficult for us to sit here and criticize the European stress tests as too weak, not sufficiently rigorous, and too opaque, when the models the Fed is using are opaque. If there's not a willingness to reveal the models beforehand and worry about gaming, there is a value I think in ex post basis so there can be legitimacy.

DOUG ELLIOTT (Brookings Institution): Paul, you expressed a preference for an accelerated legislative response rather than being so rules based. I think that's much harder to do when you're not in a parliamentary system. With our separation of powers, it's just a lot harder.

TUCKER: I said either that or change the statutory objectives of the securities regulators so that they at least have a mandate and are held accountable for the stability of those things that fall within their jurisdiction.

ELLIOTT: One of the biggest concerns about this single-point-of-entry approach that you're describing is the cross-border aspect, and some jurisdictions aren't designed with holding companies at the top. Could you talk a little bit about how to deal with that?

TUCKER: First of all, by an accident of history, the McFadden Act banned interstate banking, causing nearly all big U.S. banking groups to have peer holding companies. Out of a bad law has come a good structure in terms of resolution. That is not the case elsewhere in the world. Most of the big banks in Europe and Asia don't have peer holding companies. I believe they'll need to restructure.

This matters because what Rodgin and I are describing can sidestep an awful lot of the cross-border difficulty. Say a subsidiary in Frankfurt of a U.S. bank gets into difficulty. The subsidiary doesn't need to go into resolution or liquidation in Frankfurt. Instead, the intergroup debt can be triggered so that the subsidiary gets recapitalized. There is no default. There is no event of default in the subsidiary that is ailing. Instead, all the losses are pushed to the top of the group, and the group as a whole can be dealt with by one authority.

Now this requires host authorities to then step out of the way and allow the home authority to do that. But one of the things I like about that is for the first time in living memory, this will make home and host authorities have a concrete discussion about cooperation. This isn't to do with goodwill. They will be able to find out in black-and-white terms whether they are prepared to enter into agreements that will allow this structure to work, and if they don't make those agreements, then they will vocalize, and this will play out over the next year or two. A debate that has bedeviled banking supervision for thirty or forty years will, I believe, come to an end.

5

FEDERAL RESERVE INDEPENDENCE AFTER THE FINANCIAL CRISIS
Should We Be Worried?

DONALD KOHN

We are going through an extraordinary period in business cycles and central banking. The too-calm, too-confident veneer of the Great Moderation was shattered by the worst financial crisis in eighty years. The Federal Reserve—indeed central banks all over the industrial world—took extraordinary actions to make sure the crisis was not followed by an economic result like that of the 1930s, and they continue to pursue policies that not so long ago would have been considered unthinkable.

Naturally, understandably, and appropriately, these circumstances have increased the scrutiny of central banks and raised questions about the goals, governance, and accountability of these institutions. The issue before us is whether we should worry that this scrutiny will result in an erosion of their independence from the elected government. We should be concerned about the potential for reduced independence: evidence over time and across countries indicates that less independence is correlated with higher inflation.[1] To foreshadow my answer: the actions that the Federal Reserve and other central banks took should not and need

---

1. See Bernanke (2010) and the references in that speech.

not lead to a loss of monetary policy independence, but we need to be vigilant. The risks and threats to independence have increased.

The wisdom of a high degree of independence for central banks in the conduct of monetary policy is well established. Goals for policy are and should be set in the democratic process by elected representatives. The Federal Reserve Act, as amended in 1977, charges the Federal Reserve with pursuing "maximum employment, stable prices and moderate long-term interest rates."[2] The primary objective of the European Central Bank, by treaty, is "to maintain price stability."[3]

Independence is critical in the setting of the instruments—interest rates and the like—to achieve these goals. Central banks should be held ultimately accountable for outcomes, and not for the techniques they used to get to those outcomes. Instrument independence is necessary to overcome the short-term perspective of politicians, who tend to be more interested in boosting economic growth before the next election and less focused on the longer-term inflationary consequences of such actions. This view is widely shared around the globe, as evidenced by the lengthening lists of central banks that are, in this sense, independent of the elected government.

Of course, instrument settings are subject to public discussion and legislative hearings. That is key to holding the independent central bank accountable. The Federal Reserve or any other independent central bank needs to explain how its actions are related to the achievement of its objectives. And those discussions and hearings will involve political pressures—alternative views about interest rates or the size and composition of the central bank's balance sheet. An independent central bank—one that has been insulated from these pressures—doesn't need to follow the politicians' instructions. It should resist where those desires are inconsistent with its own views of how to achieve the objectives.

The legislative framework for monetary policy can be changed, of course, and it can be changed in ways that impinge on a central bank's instrument independence and thus its ability to achieve its mandate. Proposals to alter the Federal Reserve's mandate or its governance surface

2. For a brief history of the Federal Reserve's mandate, see Steelman (2011).

3. See Article 127, "Consolidated Version of the Treaty on the Functioning of the European Union" (http://eur-lex.europa.eu/LexUriServ/LexUriServ.do?uri=OJ:C:2012:326:0047:0200:EN:PDF).

regularly in Congress, though few have garnered substantial support and none has actually been passed since the late 1970s. But the crisis and the actions the Federal Reserve felt compelled to take during the crisis weakened public support for the institution and its independence, and led to some unusually stiff attacks from prominent politicians.

To reprise briefly, during the crisis the Federal Reserve expanded access to the discount window for banks and opened credit facilities to non-banks for the first time since the 1930s. It helped stabilize or facilitate the takeover of systemically important institutions at risk of failure that would have further disrupted the financial system. The Federal Reserve aggressively reduced short-term rates to zero and then, to spur growth, worked to reduce intermediate- and long-term rates even further by greatly expanding its balance sheet with purchases of long-term securities and by issuing guidance about the future path of short-term rates. It addressed perceived clogs in the transmission of monetary policy by intervening directly in the government-guaranteed mortgage market—taking a hand in credit allocation where markets were not functioning well. Other central banks in industrial countries that have been hit by crisis in recent years have taken comparable, unconventional steps to stabilize markets and encourage growth. We are in uncharted territory in our understanding of both economic developments and the policy response.

The old simple notion was that the Federal Reserve did monetary policy (essentially moving short-term interest rates up or down by announcing its target for these rates and intervening modestly in government securities markets to validate that target, and by serving as a very temporary—usually overnight—source of liquidity to depository institutions), and Congress and the president did fiscal policy (taxes, spending, and pretty much anything that put taxpayers' money at risk). A number of the actions the Federal Reserve took during and after the crisis straddled the line between fiscal and monetary policies. They involved taking some limited fiscal risk onto the central bank's balance sheet, and they entailed close cooperation between the monetary and fiscal authorities. This was particularly true in the depths of the crisis: when loans were made against collateral of unquestioned quality in normal markets but whose current market value was under pressure from panics, fire sales, and liquidity premiums; when, in an attempt to restart markets and calm fears, the Federal Reserve covered the tail risk of some types of assets—losses that might occur after the private sector (and sometimes the Treasury's Troubled Asset Relief Program, TARP) had already absorbed losses; when in the absence of Federal Deposit Insurance Corporation (FDIC) authority to resolve systemically important institutions, the Federal Reserve took the tail risk on special facilities to stabilize such institutions or facilitate their takeover by another private sector entity (in some cases behind the Treasury's TARP and the FDIC). Just as the distinctions between liquidity and solvency problems become much less sharp in a crisis, so, too, do the distinctions between fiscal and monetary policies designed to limit the scope of the crisis.

The Federal Reserve did not expect to take losses on any of these facilities—and all those loans were indeed repaid without any losses to the Federal Reserve or the taxpayers. And the very act of making those loans helped to limit the extent and duration of the crisis—fulfilling one of the principal rationales for the founding of the Federal Reserve 100 years ago. But had the financial panics continued and deepened and many more borrowers failed, the taxpayer could have suffered losses.

There is no doubt that the crisis elevated the public profile of the Federal Reserve; the evidence of its authority—to make loans to non-banks, to help rescue Bear Stearns and the American International Group (AIG), to backstop money market mutual funds, to buy hundreds of billions of dollars of mortgage-backed securities—startled many Americans, including members of Congress. To some, the Federal Reserve's actions challenged the essence of democracy: namely, that the people's elected representatives levy taxes and spend the money. To some extent, this discomfort reflected Congress's inability (or unwillingness) to distinguish between lending and spending—the Federal Reserve had always had an unlimited ability to do the former, which, for example, it had exercised in size after 9/11. But the reach and extent of the lending was unprecedented, and it fostered a perception that Wall Street was being favored over Main Street. The Federal Reserve itself was uncomfortable with some of its operations, urging the Treasury to seek congressional funding for any rescues that might follow AIG, and urging Congress to give the FDIC resolution authority over systemically important financial institutions in the Dodd-Frank legislation.

Coupled with the Federal Reserve's failure to prevent the crisis, these actions greatly reduced public confidence in the institution. In 2007 a

FIGURE 5-1. Confidence in Federal Reserve Board
Chairman Ben Bernanke on the Economy (2006–13)

Percent

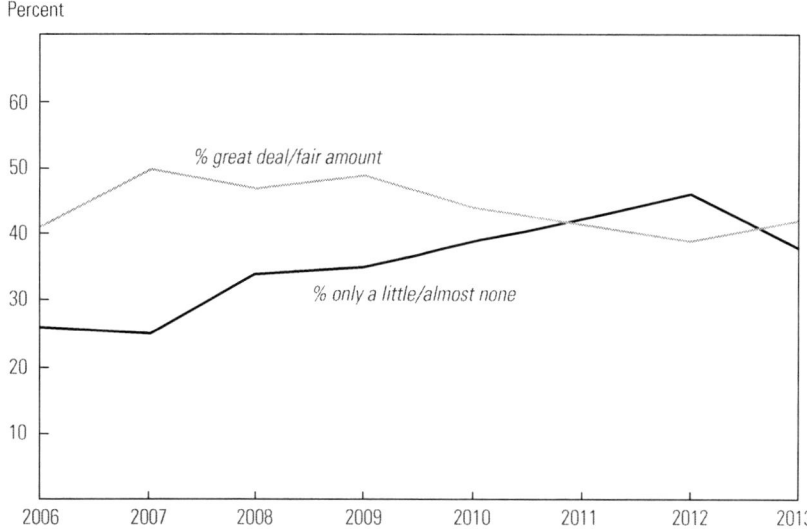

Source: "Americans Trust Obama Most on Economy," Gallup Politics, April 10, 2013 (http://www.gallup.com/poll/161723/
americans-trust-obama-economy.aspx). See also "Gallup Poll Social Series: Economy and Personal Finance," Gallup News
Service, April 4–7, 2013 (http://www.gallup.com/file/poll/161726/Who_You_Trust_%20the_Economy_130410.pdf).

Gallup poll found that 50 percent of Americans expressed a great deal
or fair amount of confidence that Ben Bernanke would do or recommend the right thing for the economy, and only 25 percent said they had
only a little confidence or almost none. (The remaining 25 percent didn't
have a view.) That confidence steadily eroded over the ensuing years. By
2012, 39 percent expressed a great deal or a fair amount of confidence
in him, and 46 percent said they had little or none. (Only 15 percent
had no opinion.) The trend lines have turned more favorable lately: an
April 2013 poll found 42 percent in the great deal/fair amount camp and
38 percent in the little/none camp (Figure 5-1).

INDEPENDENCE AND ACCOUNTABILITY

When discussing central bank independence and accountability, it's
important to make a key distinction and to recall how we have arrived
where we are.

The distinction concerns functions performed by the central bank. With regard to independence, our main focus has been on the setting of monetary policy, not regulatory policy. In this regard, the Federal Reserve has always lived with a bifurcated regime. The regulatory functions of the Federal Reserve have involved a very high degree of cooperation and coordination with other agencies. Major decisions are arrived at jointly by several agencies, and those decisions are subject to examination and oversight by the Government Accountability Office (GAO) of Congress.

The cooperative character of bank regulation is made necessary by the balkanized U.S. regulatory system, with many different agencies having a hand in regulation and supervision of the financial system. It also reflects the nature of the actions taken. Regulation is necessary to offset the moral hazard created by the safety net and to deal with externalities, but it involves elements of credit allocation, it constrains private decisions, and it affects the relative positions of individual firms. And it can have consequences for the public purse if regulation and supervision are not effective enough at constraining risk. Some degree of independence from political pressure is necessary in carrying out these tasks, but they may not lend themselves to the same arm's-length relationship to elected representatives or other parts of the executive branch as does monetary policy.

The notion that different degrees of independence can apply to different categories of central bank decisions—more for monetary policy and less for regulation—makes some people uncomfortable. They express concern that the lesser autonomy of regulation can spill over to erode the arm's-length relationship protecting monetary policy decisions from political interference. But such differences have persisted for many decades in the United States, and practitioners see them as inevitable. As Stan Fischer has noted, "Some of my colleagues say, well, you can't be independent in one role and not in another. Well, I don't think any of them are married, if that's what they say. You can be. There are things you do (separately) and there are things you do together. I don't see why you can't be independent one way and not in the other."[4]

---

4. Quoted in da Costa (2013). See also Wessel (2013).

The degree of monetary policy independence and associated account-ability has changed considerably over the past several decades. In the 1960s, in the Kennedy and Johnson administrations, belief was wide-spread that explicitly coordinating the setting of monetary and fiscal policies would result in better overall outcomes for the economy, with emphasis on promoting growth and jobs. The resulting constraints on monetary policy now are seen as the first steps in what became the "great inflation" of the 1970s. During the 1970s monetary policy became complicit in ever-rising inflation by holding back on decisive action as various administrations undertook incomes policies and jawboning of wages and prices to avoid the costs of the tough monetary policies that were needed and eventually implemented to reestablish price stability. By the end of the 1970s both experience and evolving theories of mon-etary policy effects and decisionmaking pointed to a need for monetary policy to be implemented with considerable independence from these other types of policies if inflation were to be contained.

Congressional dissatisfaction with economic outcomes and the poli-cies of the Federal Reserve resulted in legislative actions in 1977 and 1978 that established the "dual mandate" of the Federal Reserve for "stable prices" and "maximum employment," and also an account-ability structure of regular reports and hearings on monetary policy—focused initially around the growth of monetary aggregates as the instruments or intermediate targets for achieving these long-term objec-tives. And those reports contained projections from policymakers of future output, inflation, and unemployment expected to be consistent with "appropriate monetary policy."

The sustainability of a high degree of independence for instrument settings in a democracy requires the independent authority to explain what it is doing and why. In that regard, although the congressional hearings have often been a disappointing forum for examining monetary policy choices, the Federal Reserve has taken the initiative over the years to become much more transparent about its thinking on monetary pol-icy issues. In 1994 it began announcing and explaining its decisions on the day it made them, and those explanations have become much fuller over time. It sped up the production of the minutes of its meetings so the reasoning and discussion behind the decisions were available sooner. It lengthened the period of its projections. It initiated quarterly press conferences by the chair. And it spelled out its views of its responsibility for the two legs of its dual mandate and its strategy for achieving them.

To a large extent these steps were undertaken with a view to enhancing the effectiveness of policy by informing the expectations of financial market participants and the public making spending and saving plans. This is, of course, particularly important at a time when short-term interest rates are constrained by the zero lower bound and the Federal Reserve has been looking for alternative tools. To be sure, the messages have sometimes been misunderstood; both the Federal Reserve and those listening to it seem sometimes to lose sight of the inherent uncertainty around expectations for economic developments and appropriate policy responses, especially in circumstances like those prevailing in recent years, which have no real precedent in the economy, financial markets, and policy.

The additional information and transparency also play an important role in holding the central bank accountable and maintaining its instrument independence. As Chairman Bernanke put it recently,

> One of my personal objectives since I became Chairman has been to increase the transparency of the Fed—to more clearly explain how our policies are intended to work and the thinking behind our decisions. . . . [I]mproved communication can help our policies work better, whether through the disclosure of bank stress-test results or by helping the public and market participants better understand how monetary policy is likely to evolve. Ultimately, however, the most important reason for transparency and clear communication is to help ensure the accountability of our independent institution to the American people and their elected representatives. Clarity, transparency, and accountability help build public confidence in the Federal Reserve, which is essential if it is to be successful in fostering stability and prosperity.[5]

THREATS TO INDEPENDENCE

In considering whether Federal Reserve independence is likely to be threatened by the nature and aggressive character of its recent actions,

---

5. Bernanke (2013).

it's important to keep in mind that there is no necessary connection between recent actions and future loss of independence. This is a decision for Congress to make, and it needs to understand the costs and benefits from any erosion of independence. Moreover, concern about a potential mistake by Congress in this regard is not a reason for the Federal Reserve to hold back on using the tools Congress has given it to accomplish the objectives Congress has set. The Federal Reserve needs to keep explaining why it considers its actions to have been consistent with furthering its objectives, and that any fiscal risk incurred or credit allocation affected by its actions has been necessary to achieve its legislated objectives and has been a temporary function of an extraordinary situation. We can see from what has occurred in Japan that perceptions of timidity and caution also have the potential to bring unusually intense political pressures to bear on a nominally independent central bank. The view that monetary policy needed to be much more aggressive and innovative was a central issue in the campaign of late 2012 in Japan, and the winning candidate appointed a new governor, whose policy innovations are characterized as one "arrow" in the government's overall economic strategy.

A number of risk factors suggest extra vigilance will be called for over the coming years to preserve the appropriate degree of Federal Reserve independence.

First, an era of polarization of political discourse has not proven conducive to a reasoned discussion of monetary policy and the pros and cons of independence. Exhibit 1 in this regard would be the debates in the Republican primaries with candidates competing as to how rapidly they would "fire" Ben Bernanke, with one characterizing a policy disagreement as "almost treasonous."[6] Also discouraging was the unprecedented letter from the four top Republican congressional leaders to the Federal Reserve in September 2011 trying to dictate an instrument setting—the management of its portfolio.[7] Although Ben Bernanke was, at least nominally, a Republican before coming to Washington, was appointed to the Federal Reserve Board by President George W. Bush, and served as the chair of Bush's Council of Economic Advisers, the

---

6. Perry (2011).
7. "Full Text: Republicans' Letter to Bernanke Questioning More Fed Action," *Wall Street Journal*, September 20, 2011 (http://blogs.wsj.com/economics/2011/09/20/full-text-republicans-letter-to-bernanke-questioning-more-fed-action/).

FIGURE 5-2. Confidence in Federal Reserve Board Chairman
Ben Bernanke on the Economy (2006–13): Percent Expressing
Great Deal/Fair Amount by Party Affiliation

Percent

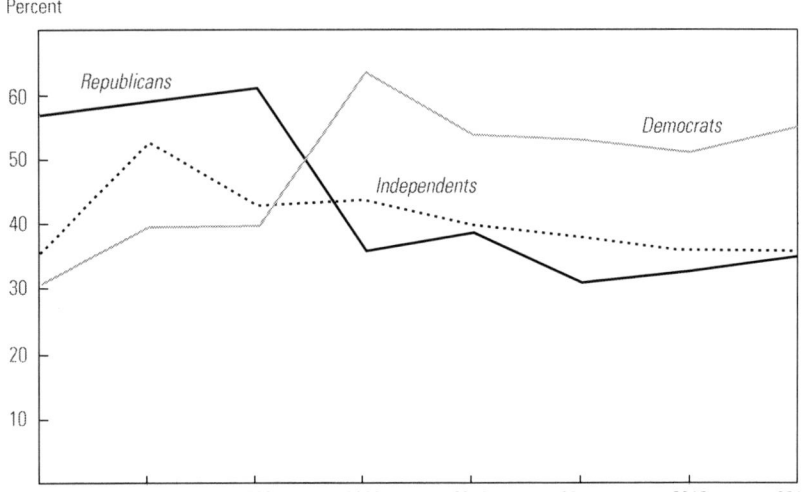

Source: "Americans Trust Obama Most on Economy," Gallup Politics, April 10, 2013 (http://www.gallup.com/poll/161723/
americans-trust-obama-economy.aspx). See also "Gallup Poll Social Series: Economy and Personal Finance," Gallup News
Service, April 4–7, 2013 (http://www.gallup.com/file/poll/161726/Who_You_Trust_%20the_Economy_130410.pdf).

antipathy to him and his actions has been markedly partisan. An April
2013 Gallup poll found 55 percent of self-identified Democrats but only
36 percent of Republicans express a great deal or a fair amount of confidence in Bernanke (see figure 5-2).[8] Before the crisis, it was the other
way around. The Senate vote on his confirmation for a second term as
chair in 2010 was 70–30, with only five Republicans supporting him.
Paul Volcker was confirmed 98–0 in 1979 and 84–16 in 1983. Alan
Greenspan's confirmation votes were 91–2, unanimous, 91–7, 89–4,
and a voice vote in which only one senator asked to be recorded as vot-
ing "no" (table 5-1). As I'll underline in a second, we haven't yet heard
from the forces that might eventually be aroused by exit from today's
unconventional monetary policies and very low interest rates.

8. "Americans Trust Obama Most on Economy," Gallup Politics, April 10, 2013 (www.
gallup.com/poll/161723/americans-trust-obama-economy.aspx).

TABLE 5-1. Confirmation Votes, Federal Reserve Chair

Nominee	Year	Votes
Paul Volcker	1979	98–0
Paul Volcker	1983	84–16
Alan Greenspan	1987	91–2
Alan Greenspan	1992	Uncontested (voice vote)
Alan Greenspan	1996	91–7
Alan Greenspan	2000	89–4
Alan Greenspan	2004	Uncontested (voice vote)
Ben Bernanke	2006	Uncontested (voice vote)
Ben Bernanke	2010	70–30
Janet Yellen	2014	56–26

Source: Gregory Giroux, "Bloomberg by the Numbers: 70," Bloomberg, December 20, 2013 (http://go.bloomberg.com/political-capital/2013-12-20/bloomberg-by-the-numbers-70-4/).

Second, the Federal Reserve has had some powers trimmed in the Dodd-Frank measures, suggesting that the erosion of trust and deference illustrated by the polls and confirmation votes can have implications for Federal Reserve authority. The restrictions apply to its authority to lend to non-bank institutions under Section 13-3 of the Federal Reserve Act and include an obligation to get the approval of the secretary of the Treasury even for widely available facilities. In addition, against the recommendation of the Federal Reserve, the Congress mandated the publication of the names of all borrowers at the discount window—bank and non-bank—no later than two years after they borrow. So far, the instrument independence of the Federal Reserve in monetary policy per se has not been abridged in any way, but it may be that the Federal Reserve's views carry less weight than they did before the crisis. Third, although in recent years the political blowback mainly has come from those who say they are worried about inflation, the major challenge to independence is likely to come from those concerned about unemployment as the Federal Reserve exits from unconventional policies. At some point the Federal Reserve will need to tighten policy to keep inflation from rising persistently above its 2 percent inflation target. It will need to raise rates and begin returning its portfolio toward its prior plain-vanilla size and composition. The decision to turn toward tightening is always difficult and subject to second-guessing in the political sphere. It will be even tougher after a long period of weak growth, unprecedented policy actions, and historically low mortgage and other interest rates.

It will be a complex exit involving many steps—with lots of opportunity for kibitzing and objecting over a long period. It will ultimately involve a sharp correction in long-term rates—an increase in term premiums as well as an upward adjustment in expected short-term rates. It will entail withdrawal of special support for the mortgage market. As long-term rates rise, the Federal Reserve will have mark-to-market losses on its balance sheet. These losses are not a threat to the Federal Reserve's ability to tighten nor do they have any economic significance, but losses could be used as a political weapon by those who seek to curtail the Federal Reserve's independence or limit its powers. A main tightening tool will be increases in the interest rate paid to banks on their deposits at the Federal Reserve, further damping Federal Reserve profits. This is a tool well known in other jurisdictions, but it is new for the United States. It could fuel accusations that the Federal Reserve is doing favors for the big banks. The size of the portfolio shouldn't impede the ability to tighten, given this new tool, but a huge volume of reserves could make control over the federal funds rate less precise than it has been in the past. Finally, in light of the apparent inability of Congress and the administration to deal with longer-term budget issues, the rise in rates could be occurring in the context of a still-unsustainable path for budget and debt, and higher rates will underline that issue and make it worse. This will be another source of unhappiness in the political sphere.

Fourth, the Federal Reserve, like many other central banks, has been given added responsibilities in regulation and supervision. These responsibilities include a key role in macroprudential regulation, with responsibility for protecting the overall stability of the financial system. Carrying out this regulation already involves a differential impact on some organizations—those identified as systemically important. It could also entail tightening up regulation when credit is growing too fast and financial imbalances are seen to be developing—another form of taking away the punch bowl as the party gets going—for example, through raising the countercyclical capital buffer under Basel III. This will not be popular with those drinking the punch. In the years leading up to the crisis, we saw considerable political resistance to even mild forms of tighter supervisory policy, for example, with respect to commercial real estate lending. The risk is that greater scrutiny and criticism of this aspect of Federal Reserve activity could spill over to monetary policy. It is important to retain the bifurcation—the differences in governance and accountability for regulation and monetary policy.

But macroprudential policy could also protect monetary policy independence and the flexibility to achieve its objectives. It reduces the need for the Federal Reserve to use monetary policy to deal with bubbles, imbalances, or a buildup of leverage. It now has another set of tools to apply to these. Monetary policy can be focused on price stability and maximum employment and more readily held accountable for those less diffuse goals than for "financial stability." More focused goals and accountability should support retaining monetary policy independence. In the United Kingdom, the Monetary Policy Committee (MPC) has put in place forward guidance on interest rates very similar to that in the United States. But it has accompanied this forward guidance with a "knock out" for the Financial Policy Committee (FPC)—the macro-prudential authority. If the FPC sees a threat to financial stability from the low interest rates of the MPC, it can knock out the pledge of the MPC to maintain those very low rates until after unemployment reaches 7 percent, but only after the FPC has tried the other tools available to it to deal with the financial stability threat. Thus each committee is held responsible for achieving its particular objectives, using as far as possible the instruments at its disposal.

The most immediate threat to appropriate independence now would seem to be the perennial proposal to allow the GAO to audit monetary policy, removing an exemption that has existed since the 1970s. The expanded GAO audit authority to review and critique monetary policy decisions would be another avenue to bring pressure on the setting of the Federal Reserve's monetary policy instruments. Of course, such pressure can and should be ignored when the Federal Reserve is convinced it is doing the right thing to accomplish its legislated objectives. But extending the GAO audit moves the needle, however slightly, in the wrong direction when it will be important to protect the Federal Reserve's instrument independence as it exits from unconventional monetary policies and ultra-low interest rates. It erodes the distinction between the governance of regulatory and monetary policy functions that seems so useful to make.

Preserving the Federal Reserve's monetary policy independence will be critical over the next few years. There's just too much history that shows that less independence leads to higher inflation over time.

REFERENCES

Bernanke, Ben. 2010. "Central Bank Independence, Transparency, and Accountability." Speech presented to Institute for Monetary and Economic Studies International Conference, Tokyo, Japan, May 25 (www.federalreserve.gov/newsevents/speech/bernanke20100525a.htm).

———. 2013. "Opening Remarks." Ceremony Commemorating the Centennial of the Federal Reserve Act, Washington, D.C., December 16 (www.federal reserve.gov/newsevents/speech/bernanke20131216a.htm).

Da Costa, Pedro. 2013. "Central Bank Independence Is a Bit Like Marriage: Israel's Fisher." Reuters (April 18) (http://blogs.reuters.com/macroscope/2013/04/18/central-bank-independence-is-a-bit-like-marriage-israels-fischer/).

Giroux, Gregory. 20213. "Bloomberg by the Numbers: 70." Bloomberg (December 20) (http://go.bloomberg.com/political-capital/2013-12-20/bloomberg-by-the-numbers-70-4/).

Perry, Rick. 2011. "Printing Money Is 'Almost Treasonous,'" Video (August 15) (www.youtube.com/watch?v=goAj388gngI).

Steelman, Aaron. 2011. "The Federal Reserve's 'Dual Mandate': The Evolution of an Idea." Federal Reserve Bank of Richmond (December) (www.richmondfed.org/publications/research/economic_brief/2011/pdf/eb_11-12.pdf).

Wessel, David. 2013. "Are Central Banks Putting Their Independence at Risk?" *Wall Street Journal*, April 17 (http://blogs.wsj.com/economics/2013/04/17/are-central-banks-putting-their-independence-at-risk/).

DISCUSSION

Responding to Donald Kohn's presentation were two prominent academic economists, Christina Romer of the University of California at Berkeley and Kenneth Rogoff of Harvard University.

ROMER: I agree completely with what Don Kohn said about the fundamental importance of central bank independence and the threats to the Fed, but for a different reason. I think that a somewhat different perspective on why central bank independence matters gives you a different sense of where the threats are coming from.

Don gives a classic case for central bank independence. Politicians have a short-term outlook—they just want to win elections—and if you let them control monetary policy, they're going to pump up the economy before an election, and that's going to tend to cause inflation. In contrast, if you delegate monetary policy to an independent central bank, it can take a longer-run view, and then you get less of these problems, you get less inflation.

I'm skeptical of that story for a couple of reasons. A number of people have tried to look for a political business cycle and evidence that politicians do pump up the economy before elections. But they cannot find evidence of this, with the not at all surprising exception of Richard Nixon.

If you doubt my skepticism about this usual story, I just point out the bizarre situation that we find ourselves in today. In both the United States and Europe, politicians seem to care a lot more about inflation than central bankers do right now, and a lot less about the short-run state of the economy than central bankers seem to.

My most compelling reason for not believing the story about politicians and independent central bankers having different time frames comes from history. If you look back over U.S. history, and history in many other countries, when have we made mistakes? When has inflation gotten too high? When have we done other things wrong? It's not been particularly correlated with central bank independence; it's been correlated with ideas. When we go wrong is when we have screwy ideas about how the economy operates.

This leads me to think that the main reason or rationale for central bank independence is expertise. We want to delegate our monetary policy to an independent central bank because we think it will do better, because monetary policy is really hard, especially at the zero lower bound.

And just as you wouldn't want Congress telling your physicist how to build your nuclear arsenal, you don't want Congress telling the monetary policymakers how best to achieve price stability and maximum employment. We want monetary policy made by experts because we expect the outcomes to be better.

If I'm right and the main reason for central bank independence is expertise and monetary policy made by experts, then the biggest threat to independence is bad monetary policy decisions. Because then the central bank loses its main argument for independence: that it's better at it than other people.

I found one reference in Don's presentation—to Japan—a little hard to parse. I couldn't quite tell if he was lamenting that the democratically elected government had replaced the governor of the Bank of Japan, and strong-armed more expansionary monetary policy. But I think fifteen years of deflation had caused the Bank of Japan to lose its right to claim superior expertise.

An even more compelling example comes from the 1930s. In the Great Depression, the Federal Reserve thought it was taking actions that were consistent with what was written down in the Federal Reserve Act, yet its policies were failing miserably. In that situation, it's only natural that central bank independence comes under threat. At some point, accountability has to involve more than just the central bank providing information about why it's doing things. If it's failing dramatically, elected officials should take appropriate actions to fix the situation.

If the biggest threat to Fed independence is poor policy, I end up exactly where Don is, which is that the biggest counter to that threat is good policy. If the Fed or some other central bank doesn't take actions that it thinks or knows to be correct because it's afraid of how Congress will react, that's just going to be a disaster. That is going to tend to lower their independence rather than strengthen it. I had exactly the same analogy that Don had: the best defense against the threat to independence is an offense in the form of good policy.

To end up on the last point that Don made—his concern about political partisanship—again, I take it in a little bit of a different direction.

The thing that worries me most about rising partisanship is a decreasing support or belief in the value of expert opinion. And we see this not just with monetary policy, but with fiscal policy and with climate policy. We're seeing this across the board.

Some of the decline in the support for experts on monetary policy can be countered by the Federal Reserve doing an even better job of explaining why it does what it does, like compelling testimony. And here's where Chairman Ben Bernanke has made great strides—the greater transparency of the Fed under his watch will be one of his lasting contributions.

The battle needs to be fought much more broadly—by the press, by academics, and by ordinary voters. And it's fabulous that we have the Hutchins Center, because that's going to be another voice fighting for the importance of expert opinion. Only if we reestablish the value of expertise and evidence-based policymaking, can we squelch what I see as the fundamental challenge to Fed independence and to good policymaking.

DAVID WESSEL: In an era where everything has to be boiled down to a 140-character tweet, the point is independence, but only for intelligent central banks.

ROMER: That's a fine tweet.

ROGOFF: Let me pick up where Christy left off. In this world where debates become increasingly partisan—and both "expert opinion" and, in general, the center, have been destroyed and drowned out—it's a pleasure to be here at the founding meeting of the Hutchins Center, which aspires to have nonpartisan analysis.

I agree, maybe more broadly, with Don's presentation than you do, Christy, although I accept the points you made. It's a very understated discussion, but he expresses some pretty horrific concerns about what can happen.

If I can blend it in with John Williams's points, it candidly admits—again, in an understated way—that economists know less than they thought they did in understanding business cycles, especially today. And I would say that we absolutely need to look more at history. Everything has been focused on a couple of decades that don't tell us that much.

It's not that the models don't have financial markets; it's that they have perfect financial markets where nothing can ever go wrong, and then you don't have to study them. And, of course, they're the core of the problem that's going to take a long time to fix.

And then, the interplay of this involves the nonlinearities. Yes, graduate students are studying this. No, they won't have the answer in the next five to ten years.

We exist in a world of tremendous uncertainty, where we won't know if monetary policy had it right. When Ben Bernanke wrote his 1983 paper about the Great Depression, it was fifty years later, and there was a big rethinking of what we should have done.[9]

So I certainly come down on the side of central bank independence and expertise as being very important. It is an environment where it's difficult to preserve.

Let me just finish on a couple points. Certainly, I do think institutions' forecasting needs to be recalibrated. As John pointed out, we live in a world where we may have cycles more like we had before World War II, more often than we used to, and where we see them around the world. Carmen Reinhart and I have emphasized this point also. That may mirror back into inflation-targeting regimes, how you want to design institutions, which were fine-tuned for this more benign environment than we had before the crisis.

Lastly, there was discussion about monetary policy and fiscal policy, where it could have been inadequate. I think some of that was based on the forecasts not being correct.

I have to say my biggest disappointment in the policy response to the financial crisis has not been in either of those areas. It has really been in structural reforms. Where is our third arrow? Where are the reforms that are going to generate more long-term growth in the United States?

The Simpson-Bowles report had some good ideas about tax reform. But they didn't happen. Dodd-Frank legislation runs to 30,000 pages, but it's missing high equity ratios and such.

And, of course, having more infrastructure investment is something that all economists seemed to agree on all along, but it didn't happen nearly to the extent we hoped.

9. Ben S. Bernanke, "Non-Monetary Effects of the Financial Crisis in the Propagation of the Great Depression," Working Paper 1054 (Cambridge, Mass.: National Bureau of Economic Research, January 1983) (http://www.nber.org/papers/w1054.pdf?new_window=1).

Certainly these are problems that need to be studied holistically, and present challenges, because the Fed gets blamed for everything.

WESSEL: Don says the evidence is that central banks have to be independent, because otherwise we get a lot of inflation because the politicians are shortsighted. Christy says it's a nice thought, but it's not supported by the evidence. Ken, do you have a side in this?

ROGOFF: Well, of course it's better to have expertise. The Federal Reserve made mistakes in the Great Depression because it had almost no expertise. But if you ask any central banker, there are 99, or maybe 999, pressures for lower interest rates compared to higher interest rates. And something I'd echo in Don's discussion is that if you think that there were complaints about the policy now, wait until the Fed has to tighten.

ROMER: Actually, could I disagree with that for a second? Listen to some of the pressure coming out of Congress today. I'm sure there will be pressure from that direction when the Fed tries to raise rates, but there are a lot of people in Congress who are chomping at the bit for the Fed to tighten and dial back a lot on extraordinary measures. The pressures may be more balanced than you two think.

KOHN: In my experience sitting behind chairmen for about thirty years, there were many more in Congress arguing for lower rates, or not raising rates, than there were arguing for raising them.

ROMER: That gets back to "maybe the world has changed." We have to be a little careful not to be fighting the last wars, and to know where the pressures are today.

ANDY LEVIN (International Monetary Fund): One way to think about this is that in normal times, you may have a doctor that you see occasionally, and if you think he's doing a good job, you keep going to the same doctor. And, if not, you switch. The goal is to be healthy, and the instrument is the doctor figuring out what to do on a regular basis.

When you're in unusual circumstances, as when your child is sick and may have to have surgery, you'll want to consult much more closely with the physician, maybe with multiple physicians, and talk through the strategy—what type of surgery, what other sorts of treatment could be appropriate—and be much more involved in those decisions.

When it comes to the day of the surgery, in the operating room, the doctor and the other assistants have to be able to use the scalpels and decide how long the surgery is going to take, so there is a level of instrument independence.

These distinctions are what we're seeing today in the political world. We've been in a situation for the past five years that's more like a sick child, where the parents are very concerned, and where there are tough decisions: which surgery, what are the risks, and so forth.

KOHN: I agree. Part of the accountability is not so clear-cut. Congress has given very vague goals—maximum employment and stable prices—and it's been up to the Federal Reserve, which has done a good job, particularly in the past few years, defining those goals a little better so it can be held more accountable for them.

But the Fed has also done more about defining the strategy. I completely agree that part of the accountability is consulting on the strategy, explaining how the strategy is supposed to achieve the objectives, and what the risks are on either side. And under Chairman Bernanke the Fed made huge strides in that direction.

But will there be challenges for Chair Janet Yellen? You bet. And there is more to be done. That communication and consultation are definitely part of preserving independence.

ABOUT THE PARTICIPANTS

LIAQUAT AHAMED is the Pulitzer Prize–winning author of *Lords of Finance: The Bankers Who Broke the World* and a member of the Board of Trustees at the Brookings Institution. He is the former CEO of Fischer Francis Trees and Watts. Previously, he headed the World Bank's investment division.

BEN S. BERNANKE is a Distinguished Fellow in Residence at the Hutchins Center on Fiscal and Monetary Policy at the Brookings Institution. At the time of the center's inaugural, Ben Bernanke was in his final month as chairman of the Board of Governors of the Federal Reserve, a post he held from 2006 until 2014.

H. RODGIN COHEN is senior chairman of Sullivan & Cromwell, a practice that focuses on commercial banking and financial institutions. Sullivan & Cromwell played a large part in many of the financial deals during the 2008–09 financial crisis. Cohen is also vice chairman of the Economic Studies Council at the Brookings Institution.

MARTIN FELDSTEIN is the George F. Baker Professor of Economics at Harvard University and the president emeritus of the National Bureau of Economic Research, where he served as president and chief executive officer from 1978 through 2008. He was also chairman of Ronald Reagan's Council of Economic Advisers from 1982 until 1984.

TED GAYER is the vice president and director of the Economic Studies program and the Joseph A. Pechman Senior Fellow at the Brookings Institution. He conducts research on a variety of economic issues, focusing particularly on public finance, environmental and energy economics, housing, and regulatory policy.

GLENN H. HUTCHINS is a cofounder and managing director of Silver Lake, one of the world's largest firms investing in technology and technology-enabled businesses. Hutchins also serves as the vice chair of the Board of Trustees at the Brookings Institution and is on the board of the Federal Reserve Bank of New York.

DONALD KOHN is a senior fellow in Economic Studies at the Brookings Institution. He was formerly the vice chairman of the Board of Governors of the Federal Reserve System from 2006 until 2010, where he advised Ben Bernanke through the 2008–09 financial crisis. He also served as a key adviser to Alan Greenspan during his tenure as Fed chairman.

KENNETH ROGOFF is Thomas D. Cabot Professor of Public Policy and Professor of Economics at Harvard University. He was formerly the chief economist at the International Monetary Fund. His most recent book (with Carmen Reinhart), *This Time Is Different: Eight Centuries of Financial Folly*, is a *New York Times*, Amazon, and international bestseller.

CHRISTINA ROMER is Garff B. Wilson Professor of Economics at the University of California at Berkeley. She chaired Barack Obama's Council of Economic Advisers in his first term and coauthored the administration's plan for recovery from the 2008–09 financial crisis.

STROBE TALBOTT is president of the Brookings Institution and an expert on U.S. foreign policy, with specialties on Europe, Russia, South Asia, and nuclear arms control. He was deputy secretary of state in the Clinton administration.

PAUL TUCKER is a senior fellow both at Harvard's Kennedy School of Government and the Harvard Business School. Before that, he served as the deputy governor at the Bank of England, with responsibility for financial stability. He also served on the Bank's Monetary Policy Committee from 2002 until 2013 and the Financial Policy Committee in 2013.

DAVID WESSEL is the director of the Hutchins Center on Fiscal and Monetary Policy and a senior fellow in Economic Studies at the Brookings Institution. He is also a contributing correspondent to the *Wall Street Journal,* where he was on staff for thirty years, most recently as economics editor, and wrote the weekly "Capital" column.

JOHN C. WILLIAMS is the president and chief executive officer of the Federal Reserve Bank of San Francisco, a post he has held since March 2011. Previously, he was the executive vice president and director of research for the San Francisco Bank, which he joined in 2002, and an economist at the Board of Governors since 1994.

CPSIA information can be obtained at www.ICGtesting.com
Printed in the USA
BVOW07s0558180614

356686BV00003B/182/P